YASIR ARAFAT

MENACHEM BEGIN

TONY BLAIR

GEORGE W. BUSH

JIMMY CARTER

VICENTE FOX

SADDAM HUSSEIN

HOSNI MUBARAK

VLADIMIR PUTIN

MOHAMMED REZA PAHLAVI

ANWAR SADAT

THE SAUDI ROYAL FAMILY

Menachem Begin

Virginia Brackett

CHELSEA HOUSE
PUBLISHERS
A Haights Cross Communications Company

Philadelphia

CHELSEA HOUSE PUBLISHERS

EDITOR IN CHIEF Sally Cheney
DIRECTOR OF PRODUCTION Kim Shinners
CREATIVE MANAGER Takeshi Takahashi
MANUFACTURING MANAGER Diann Grasse

Staff for MENACHEM BEGIN

EDITOR Lee Marcott
ASSOCIATE EDITOR Bill Conn
PRODUCTION ASSISTANT Jaimie Winkler
PICTURE RESEARCH 21st Century Publishing and Communications, Inc.
SERIES AND COVER DESIGNER Takeshi Takahashi
LAYOUT 21st Century Publishing and Communications, Inc.

A Haights Cross Communications Company

http://www.chelseahouse.com

First Printing

1 3 5 7 9 8 6 4 2

Library of Congress Cataloging-in-Publication Data applied for.

Brackett, Virginia.
  Menachem Begin / Virginia Brackett.
    p. cm.—(Major world leaders)
Includes index.
  ISBN 0-7910-6946-X
  1. Begin, Menachem, 1913–   —Juvenile literature. 2. Prime ministers—Israel—
Biography—Juvenile literature. 3. Revisionist Zionists—Poland—Biography—Juvenile
literature. 4. Israel—Politics and government—Juvenile literature. I. Title. II. Series.
DS126.6.B33 B73 2002
956.9405'4'092—dc21

                                                                    2002008258

TABLE OF CONTENTS

Foreword: On Leadership
Arthur M. Schlesinger, jr.   6

1   The Third Greatest Day   13

2   Terrorist or Freedom Fighter?   25

3   The Power of the Party   37

4   A New Prime Minister:
    A Renewed Vision   51

5   Peace and Fame   63

6   A Time of Dissent   75

7   An Aged Warrior   89

8   Menachem Begin's Legacy   97

    Chronology   100
    Further Reading   102
    Index   103

On Leadership

Arthur M. Schlesinger, jr.

Leadership, it may be said, is really what makes the world go round. Love no doubt smoothes the passage; but love is a private transaction between consenting adults. Leadership is a public transaction with history. The idea of leadership affirms the capacity of individuals to move, inspire, and mobilize masses of people so that they act together in pursuit of an end. Sometimes leadership serves good purposes, sometimes bad; but whether the end is benign or evil, great leaders are those men and women who leave their personal stamp on history.

Now, the very concept of leadership implies the proposition that individuals can make a difference. This proposition has never been universally accepted. From classical times to the present day, eminent thinkers have regarded individuals as no more than the agents and pawns of larger forces, whether the gods and goddesses of the ancient world or, in the modern era, race, class, nation, the dialectic, the will of the people, the spirit of the times, history itself. Against such forces, the individual dwindles into insignificance.

So contends the thesis of historical determinism. Tolstoy's great novel *War and Peace* offers a famous statement of the case. Why, Tolstoy asked, did millions of men in the Napoleonic Wars, denying their human feelings and their common sense, move back and forth across Europe slaughtering their fellows? "The war," Tolstoy answered, "was bound to happen simply because it was bound to happen." All prior history determined it. As for leaders, they, Tolstoy said, "are but the labels that serve to give a name to an end and, like labels, they have the least possible connection with the event." The greater the leader, "the more conspicuous the inevitability and the predestination of every act he commits." The leader, said Tolstoy, is "the slave of history."

Determinism takes many forms. Marxism is the determinism of class. Nazism the determinism of race. But the idea of men and women as the slaves of history runs athwart the deepest human instincts. Rigid determinism abolishes the idea of human freedom—the assumption of free choice that underlies every move we make, every word we speak, every thought we think. It abolishes the idea of human responsibility, since it is manifestly unfair to reward or punish people for actions that are by definition beyond their control. No one can live consistently by any deterministic creed. The Marxist states prove this themselves by their extreme susceptibility to the cult of leadership.

More than that, history refutes the idea that individuals make no difference. In December 1931 a British politician crossing Fifth Avenue in New York City between 76th and 77th Streets around 10:30 P.M. looked in the wrong direction and was knocked down by an automobile—a moment, he later recalled, of a man aghast, a world aglare: "I do not understand why I was not broken like an eggshell or squashed like a gooseberry." Fourteen months later an American politician, sitting in an open car in Miami, Florida, was fired on by an assassin; the man beside him was hit. Those who believe that individuals make no difference to history might well ponder whether the next two decades would have been the same had Mario Constasino's car killed Winston Churchill in 1931 and Giuseppe Zangara's bullet killed Franklin Roosevelt in 1933. Suppose, in addition, that Lenin had died of typhus in Siberia in 1895 and that Hitler had been killed on the western front in 1916. What would the 20th century have looked like now?

For better or for worse, individuals do make a difference. "The notion that a people can run itself and its affairs anonymously," wrote the philosopher William James, "is now well known to be the silliest of absurdities. Mankind does nothing save through initiatives on the part of inventors, great or small, and imitation by the rest of us—these are the sole factors in human progress. Individuals of genius show the way, and set the patterns, which common people then adopt and follow."

Leadership, James suggests, means leadership in thought as well as in action. In the long run, leaders in thought may well make the greater difference to the world. "The ideas of economists and political philosophers, both when they are right and when they are wrong," wrote John Maynard Keynes, "are more powerful than is commonly understood. Indeed the world is ruled by little else. Practical men, who believe themselves to be quite exempt from any intellectual influences, are usually the slaves of some defunct economist. . . . The power of vested interests is vastly exaggerated compared with the gradual encroachment of ideas."

But, as Woodrow Wilson once said, "Those only are leaders of men, in the general eye, who lead in action. . . . It is at their hands that new thought gets its translation into the crude language of deeds." Leaders in thought often invent in solitude and obscurity, leaving to later generations the tasks of imitation. Leaders in action—the leaders portrayed in this series—have to be effective in their own time.

And they cannot be effective by themselves. They must act in response to the rhythms of their age. Their genius must be adapted, in a phrase from William James, "to the receptivities of the moment." Leaders are useless without followers. "There goes the mob," said the French politician, hearing a clamor in the streets. "I am their leader. I must follow them." Great leaders turn the inchoate emotions of the mob to purposes of their own. They seize on the opportunities of their time, the hopes, fears, frustrations, crises, potentialities. They succeed when events have prepared the way for them, when the community is awaiting to be aroused, when they can provide the clarifying and organizing ideas. Leadership completes the circuit between the individual and the mass and thereby alters history.

It may alter history for better or for worse. Leaders have been responsible for the most extravagant follies and most monstrous crimes that have beset suffering humanity. They have also been vital in such gains as humanity has made in individual freedom, religious and racial tolerance, social justice, and respect for human rights.

There is no sure way to tell in advance who is going to lead for good and who for evil. But a glance at the gallery of men and women in MAJOR WORLD LEADERS suggests some useful tests.

One test is this: Do leaders lead by force or by persuasion? By command or by consent? Through most of history leadership was exercised by the divine right of authority. The duty of followers was to defer and to obey. "Theirs not to reason why/Theirs but to do and die." On occasion, as with the so-called enlightened despots of the 18th century in Europe, absolutist leadership was animated by humane purposes. More often, absolutism nourished the passion for domination, land, gold, and conquest and resulted in tyranny.

The great revolution of modern times has been the revolution of equality. "Perhaps no form of government," wrote the British historian James Bryce in his study of the United States, *The American Commonwealth*, "needs great leaders so much as democracy." The idea that all people should be equal in their legal condition has undermined the old structure of authority, hierarchy, and deference. The revolution of equality has had two contrary effects on the nature of leadership. For equality, as Alexis de Tocqueville pointed out in his great study *Democracy in America*, might mean equality in servitude as well as equality in freedom.

"I know of only two methods of establishing equality in the political world," Tocqueville wrote. "Rights must be given to every citizen, or none at all to anyone . . . save one, who is the master of all." There was no middle ground "between the sovereignty of all and the absolute power of one man." In his astonishing prediction of 20th-century totalitarian dictatorship, Tocqueville explained how the revolution of equality could lead to the *Führerprinzip* and more terrible absolutism than the world had ever known.

But when rights are given to every citizen and the sovereignty of all is established, the problem of leadership takes a new form, becomes more exacting than ever before. It is easy to issue commands and enforce them by the rope and the stake, the concentration camp and the *gulag*. It is much harder to use argument and achievement to overcome opposition and win consent. The Founding Fathers of the United States understood the difficulty. They believed that history had given them the opportunity to decide, as Alexander Hamilton wrote in the first Federalist Paper, whether men are indeed capable of basing government on "reflection and choice, or whether they are forever destined to depend . . . on accident and force."

Government by reflection and choice called for a new style of leadership and a new quality of followership. It required leaders to be responsive to popular concerns, and it required followers to be active and informed participants in the process. Democracy does not eliminate emotion from politics; sometimes it fosters demagoguery; but it is confident that, as the greatest of democratic leaders put it, you cannot fool all of the people all of the time. It measures leadership by results and retires those who overreach or falter or fail.

It is true that in the long run despots are measured by results too. But they can postpone the day of judgment, sometimes indefinitely, and in the meantime they can do infinite harm. It is also true that democracy is no guarantee of virtue and intelligence in government, for the voice of the people is not necessarily the voice of God. But democracy, by assuring the right of opposition, offers built-in resistance to the evils inherent in absolutism. As the theologian Reinhold Niebuhr summed it up, "Man's capacity for justice makes democracy possible, but man's inclination to justice makes democracy necessary."

A second test for leadership is the end for which power is sought. When leaders have as their goal the supremacy of a master race or the promotion of totalitarian revolution or the acquisition and exploitation of colonies or the protection of greed and privilege or the preservation of personal power, it is likely that their leadership will do little to advance the cause of humanity. When their goal is the abolition of slavery, the liberation of women, the enlargement of opportunity for the poor and powerless, the extension of equal rights to racial minorities, the defense of the freedoms of expression and opposition, it is likely that their leadership will increase the sum of human liberty and welfare.

Leaders have done great harm to the world. They have also conferred great benefits. You will find both sorts in this series. Even "good" leaders must be regarded with a certain wariness. Leaders are not demigods; they put on their trousers one leg after another just like ordinary mortals. No leader is infallible, and every leader needs to be reminded of this at regular intervals. Irreverence irritates leaders but is their salvation. Unquestioning submission corrupts leaders and demeans followers. Making a cult of a leader is always a mistake. Fortunately hero worship generates its own antidote. "Every hero," said Emerson, "becomes a bore at last."

The signal benefit the great leaders confer is to embolden the rest of us to live according to our own best selves, to be active, insistent, and resolute in affirming our own sense of things. For great leaders attest to the reality of human freedom against the supposed inevitabilities of history. And they attest to the wisdom and power that may lie within the most unlikely of us, which is why Abraham Lincoln remains the supreme example of great leadership. A great leader, said Emerson, exhibits new possibilities to all humanity. "We feed on genius . . . . Great men exist that there may be greater men."

Great leaders, in short, justify themselves by emancipating and empowering their followers. So humanity struggles to master its destiny, remembering with Alexis de Tocqueville: "It is true that around every man a fatal circle is traced beyond which he cannot pass; but within the wide verge of that circle he is powerful and free; as it is with man, so with communities." ■

After thirteen days of negotiations, U.S. President Jimmy Carter (center), Egyptian President Anwar Sadat (left), and Israeli Prime Minister Menachem Begin (right), signed a peace treaty between Egypt and Israel.

1

The Third Greatest Day

The reporter flicked the ashes from his cigarette and sighed. He looked around at the other news people who had gathered at the White House in Washington, D.C. Some held notepads, others microphones, and others balanced cameras on their shoulders. Behind the group stood an army of vans, all filled with video equipment that would send "live feeds" to television networks where the images would immediately transmit to their audiences. Everyone waited for the same thing, a formal announcement that represented years of bargaining. Those years had come down to days, thirteen days, to be exact. That was the length of time that three of the most important men in the world had spent at Camp David, Maryland, the U.S. presidential retreat, in negotiations for peace.

Suddenly, the bored crowd came to life. The reporter heard a faint announcement, the words of the White House representative whipped away on balmy September winds. A few moments later, no doubt remained about what was happening. The three heads of state had stepped out of the door. All smiled broadly and took seats at a long wooden desk, placed outside for the occasion. Behind them, a large American flag snapped in the breeze.

The reporter shaded his eyes as he moved about in the crowd, stretching to see the historic act taking place before him. Two of the men he had seen before, Jimmy Carter, President of the United States, and Anwar Sadat, President of Egypt. But on this 17th day of September 1978, he would see for the first time Menachem Begin. Begin served as prime minister of Israel, a country that had existed as a political state only since 1948. The reporter observed a balding, frail man with glasses, hardly a vision of strength. And yet he had accomplished much for his country.

Begin had come to Washington to meet with Sadat to reach a peace plan between Israel and Egypt, encouraged by President Carter. Religion played an important part in centuries-old disagreements between the countries of Israel and Egypt, both of which originated in the ancient mid-eastern country of Palestine. Israel was a Jewish country, its religion founded on an ancient Hebrew code. Egypt, like other Arab countries that surrounded tiny Israel, was populated primarily by Muslims, a group that adopted a religion called Islam. Carter's own born-again Christian faith added yet another religious twist to the negotiations. These heads of state each represented one of the three major world religions that believed in a single god—Judaism, Islam, and Christianity.

Everyone said that Carter detested Menachem Begin. There was even a rumor that President Carter's National Security Adviser, Dr. Zbigniew Brzezinski, told First Lady Rosalynn Carter that Begin was "a psycho." Begin was said to have referred to Carter as a "fanatic Baptist preacher." Fortunately, both Carter and Begin felt more positively toward Sadat.

The reporter recalled that Begin had made a lot of people the world over mad when he would not commit to returning to the Arabs some of the land that Israel took in the 1967 Six-Day war. When Israeli troops captured the Arab part of the city of Jerusalem, the Israelis declared it their capital. Arab governments and the United Nations would not acknowledge a united Jerusalem. But when Begin later became prime minister, he supported that capture and others. He had the reputation of being a bulldog when defending Israel and Judaism, and many of his own people seemed devoted to him. He had practically come back from the dead after a major heart attack to win the 1977 election. Begin remained determined to continue his lifelong promotion of "Eretz Israel," or the united land of Israel.

The reporter watched the men shake hands as they spoke to the press. They seemed tired, but pleased. As President Carter turned toward the microphone, the reporter flipped open his notebook and pulled out his pen, ready to take notes. His gaze, however, remained on Prime Minister Begin, and he wondered about the man and this peace negotiation.

During its short life of only thirty years, Israel had faced a lot of threats. Now it seemed this ordinary looking man had taken care of at least one of those threats. Still, one had to wonder whether the fragile peace could hold. The Jews had struggled for centuries to survive, overcoming threat after threat. Even though their country on the eastern shore of the Mediterranean Sea lay surrounded by enemies, it continued to thrive. At the White House signing, Begin announced that, after the birth of the State of Israel in 1948 and the uniting of Jerusalem in 1967, this was "the third greatest day of my life." No one could deny him at least partial responsibility for Israel's brief but stormy survival as a political state.

Muslim countries in the Arabian Peninsula had always surrounded the land in the present Jewish state of Israel. During Begin's time, those countries included Lebanon to the north, Syria to the northeast, Jordan to the east, and Egypt to the southwest. Long before those countries had names, however, religious differences between the people who lived in the area known as Palestine, home of the ancient Hebrew, later Jewish, kingdom, led to war and unrest. The Old Testament of the Jewish and Christian Bibles and the Islamic sacred book, the Qur'an, also known as the Koran, both tell of two sons of the Hebrew patriarch Abraham. One became important to the Islamic tradition and one important to the Jewish tradition. While Islam and Judaism share much in common, those who practice the two religions have very different beliefs. Inherent to those beliefs is that each represents God's chosen people. Thus, much of the clash among the inhabitants of ancient Palestine was based on religious conflict.

In the story of Abraham, one of Abraham's sons, Ishmael, was born to Hagar, an Egyptian servant woman. Abraham had Ishmael with Hagar during a time when his wife, Sarah, appeared unable to have children. Shortly after Ishmael's birth, however, Sarah did become pregnant with Isaac, and she turned Hagar out of the household. Hagar took Abraham's older son, Ishmael, and fled south to Arabia.

In the Islamic version of the story, Hagar was Abraham's true wife, and Ishmael the older and favorite son. Ishmael eventually became the head of 12 tribes of desert nomads, from whom Muslims claim they descend. When the Muslim prophet Mohammed appeared about 570 A.D., he founded the religion known as Islam. His teachings were gathered into the Islamic holy book, the Koran. Islam means "submission," in Arabic, and Muslim means "one who surrenders to God." Islam teaches that all worshippers of its god, Allah, belong to one community, regardless of race or nationality. Two hundred years after Islam rose to popularity in the Arabian Peninsula, it had spread to North Africa, Persia, India, and Spain. As time passed, it continued to spread across the world. Helping its spread was the Muslim openness to converts. All one must do in order to become Muslim is declare faith in Islam; no particular teaching or public ceremony is required. Islam teaches that the Christian Bible and the Hebrew holy books are also important books, but that only the Koran represents God's perfect word. It also recognizes as prophets the Jewish leader Moses and the Christian leader Jesus, believed by Christians to be God's son.

In the Jewish and Christian Old Testament version of the Abraham story, the younger son, Isaac, received the Covenant that God had made with Abraham. He would become the patriarch, or father, of the Hebrews, God's chosen people. Twelve Hebrew tribes, seen as superior to Ishmael and his descendents, would descend from Isaac. The eventual state of Israel was to be a kingdom of peace, based upon ideals established by God that would serve as a model to all nations. The terms "Judaism" and "religion" did not exist in the early Hebrew language. Abraham's descendents followed the "Halaka," Hebrew for the "way by which to walk." A code for right living was passed down orally for centuries, until it was recorded in the Talmud, the Hebrew sacred book. Eventually, the Jewish religion dispersed around the world when the Jews scattered from Israel. On some occasions, they left willingly; at other times, they were driven from their homeland by invading groups.

In the nineteenth century, some Jews desired to return to the land of their traditions and found the political state of Israel. In 1897, Theodor Herzl of Hungary founded the Zionist movement, which encouraged Jews to immigrate to

Israel and declare it a state. The immigration received a boost from the League of Nations, a group founded in 1920 to promote world peace. It granted control over Palestine, in part the home of Abraham's descendents, to Great Britain. Hoping to encourage settlement in the area, the British invited migration of Jews. The League of Nations mandate allowed both Jews and Arabs to govern their own communities. A coalition of Muslim and Christian groups against Zionism handled Arab affairs in the early decades following the mandate. The Jewish community elected a council to oversee development of Jewish culture, an activity supported by donations of money from Jews throughout the world. Between 1919 and 1923, about 35,000 Jews, most from Russia, arrived. Between 1924 and 1932, another 60,000 Jews made the journey, most of them from Poland. A few years later, in 1943, Menachem Begin arrived in the ranks of the Free Polish Army.

Menachem Wolfovitch Begin had been born on August 16, 1913 in Brest-Litovsk, part of the Russian Empire taken from Poland. In 1921, Russia returned control of the area to Poland when Menachem was eight years old. Jews living in Poland admired the Polish people's drive to again become an independent nation. But Poland had little admiration for its Jewish population. Mostly Catholic, many Poles practiced anti-Semitism, or discrimination against Jews. Jews could not take classes at school with Poles, and they had to sit in the back of university lecture halls. Many restaurants and movie theaters restricted Jewish attendance. Despite the move for a Polish nation, the Soviet Union would occupy the area again in 1939. That occupation occurred after Hitler attacked Poland, an event that would be of great significance to Menachem's family and his own future.

Menachem had heard of Zionism from his earliest days. His father, Dov Zeev Begin, gained his education in Berlin, Germany and had traveled around Europe. He represented

Theodor Herzl started the Zionist movement in 1897; this movement encouraged Jews to immigrate to Israel. A League of Nations mandate gave control of Palestine to Great Britain, and Great Britain further encouraged Jews to migrate and settle in Israel.

his own father in the trade of timber. Through those travels, Dov met other nationalists, or Jews who hoped to found a new political nation of Israel. Those who disagreed with this idea labeled people like Dov Begin "Zionist heretics." Dov was clever and resourceful, with verbal skills so sharp that he once persuaded German authorities to repair the roof of the local synagogue, a holy house for Jewish worship. Dov had never attended college, and he decided that Menachem should learn several languages, read literature, and gain a college degree, in order to support Zionism. An obedient child, Menachem did all that his father asked, including becoming an excellent chess player. He never rebelled against his father's authority or his politics. Menachem cherished his family life and would later tell a friend that he considered his mother the equivalent of a saint.

Dov could tell that Menachem, the baby of his three children, would be a fine orator and perhaps a great political leader one day. Menachem delivered his first speech at age 10. At age 12, he joined his brother and sister in a club called Hashomer Hatzair, similar to America's Boy Scouts; his first teacher in the group was his own sister, Rachel. Dov withdrew his children's membership after only one year, as Hashomer Hatzair politics did not support Zionism.

By 15 years of age, Menachem had developed an interest in the Zionist movement for young people, called Betar. Part of Betar's training included instruction in using weapons. A Russian-born Jew named Vladimir Ze'ev Jabotinsky had founded Betar. A poet and speechmaker, Jabotinsky organized Palestinian Jews against Arabs and had been in prison in British-controlled Palestine for organizing a strike in 1920. He was forced to leave Palestine by the British in 1929 following an outbreak of violence over the access of Jews to their sacred wailing wall in the city of Jerusalem. The wall was a structure visited by male Jews for worship and prayer. In August of 1929, Arabs followed the violence at the wall

These members of the Betar Zionist youth movement hold a Zionist flag and portrait of Jobotinsky. Part of Betar's training included instruction in the use of weapons.

with attacks on Jews in Hebron and Jerusalem; 133 Jews were killed and 339 wounded. Jabotinsky had called for the return of 40,000 Jews to Palestine, and young Menachem dedicated himself to Jabotinsky and his cause. He idolized Jabotinsky and considered him his political light. He would later write that Jabotinsky taught "the key is in war, . . . not begging. Our policy is not diplomacy. A war of liberation is the most glorious of all revolutions."

Begin decided to study law and apply his knowledge to the Zionist movement. In 1935, he graduated from Warsaw University with his law degree. Shortly thereafter, he became the head of Betar in Poland. The group had 70,000 members from 600 different Polish communities. They began to feel threatened by Adolf Hitler of Germany when, from 1938 to 1940, his military, the Nazis, focused on exterminating European Jews. Historians question why Begin remained in Poland, as the threat against his life and that of others Jews increased. Some believe Begin's dedication kept him there. Others say his inaction represented the same weakness Begin would show in his later service as prime minister: he simply could not decide on a course of action.

Even as the Nazis approached his home in Warsaw, Begin continued his routine, marrying in 1939. He later told of seeing and meeting seventeen-year-old Aliza (Ola) Arnold for the first time. He wrote her a one-line letter: "I saw you, my lady, for the first time, but I feel as if I have known you all my life." Later he shared his political and religious beliefs with her. He cautioned that if they married, she would live a difficult life. He declared not only would they never be wealthy, they might even face imprisonment, "for we would have to fight for Eretz Israel." Aliza agreed with all Begin told her.

They left Warsaw the next day with other members of the Betar to Vilna, Poland. When Aliza became ill, Begin wanted to return her to her parents' home, but she refused, insisting that she accompany him. Supposedly, he and Aliza had visas, or travel permission, to enter Palestine, but he gave them to a friend. According to Begin, Aliza responded by saying, "Never mind. We'll go another time."

Menachem and Aliza settled into Vilna, but before long, he received a call to report to the local Municipality, or government office. The note read, "You are invited to call at the Municipality, Room No. 23, between the hours of 9 and 11 a.m. in connection with your application." Begin had not submitted any application. Soon he discovered that various people around him also received such "invitations." Begin suspected that, should he answer his, he would be immediately arrested. He chose instead to wait and would later write, "The N.K.V.D. [secret police] finally did 'succeed' in arresting me—although not according to plan."

Adolf Hitler and members of the Nazi Party are seen here walking in front of the Eiffel Tower in Paris, France. Begin was sent to prison during World War II, and as many as six million Jew were exterminated by the Nazis during this time.

2

Terrorist
or Freedom
Fighter?

B efore long, Begin noticed various people watching his house and following him everywhere he went. They did not even attempt to hide what they were doing. He felt concerned with his and Aliza's well being, and even more concerned about his father, brother and sister. The Nazis inflicted terrible suffering on millions of people. First Paris fell to the German invasion, and then all of France surrendered. Hitler and his henchman, Himmler, sealed the doom of millions of Jews, many of whom were trapped in the Russian regime. As Begin wrote, "catastrophe followed catastrophe. And in the midst of all these catastrophes, both private and national . . . Ze'ev Jabotinsky died." At his death in 1940, Jabotinsky had been in New York, hoping to gain support for Zionism. Begin continued, "I felt that the bearer of hope was gone, never to return; and with him—perhaps never to return—hope itself."

Because of the suffering that surrounded Begin, he did not feel anxious when the secret police did at last come to his house. By that time, he was overwhelmed by "a sea of suffering, deep and wide as the ocean . . . It was not the suffering of living. . . . it was the suffering of stark fear, the suffering of people trapped by those who seek to annihilate them." He at first debated with the two policemen, using his knowledge of law, demanding a warrant for his arrest. The secret police replied as Begin anticipated. They had no warrant, but they did have the power to arrest him. They told Begin he would not need any of his possessions, as he would soon return home. The police permitted Aliza to escort Begin to the car, and he said goodbye to a few friends that he saw along the way.

Begin faced several questioning sessions, or interrogations, by "friendly" police. He knew that he would never leave the jail, and could only take satisfaction in closely observing the secret workings of the N.K.V.D. He quickly determined their routine in their "interviews." They never labeled the "invitee" a prisoner and never produced a warrant for arrest. Should the "invitee" cooperate and supply the desired answers, generally identifying his friends and neighbors as possible enemies of the state, he would be allowed to return home. As time passed, however, people came to understand that freedom would be brief; they would always receive additional "invitations." When asked to write the "truth" about his life, Begin questioned whether he should write in Polish or Yiddish, a language derived mainly from German and Hebrew often spoken by eastern-European Jews. His interrogator replied that the government office could translate from many languages, but he preferred Yiddish, because, "I am a Jew, too." When Begin expressed surprise, the questioner added, "as a Jew you can trust me."

After writing out his life's history, Begin returned to his cell and received no food or drink. A guard took away his books, and he had to sit facing a wall for the next sixty hours while authorities "reviewed" his history. His knees forced against the wall,

Begin could not alter his position or manage much sleep, but he felt lucky. Other "invitees" had to stand or walk as they waited. Later released from isolation and taken to a cell, he met several fellow prisoners in the "Lukishki," or jail. Many had been there for weeks, and they begged him for news of the outside world.

While in jail, Begin continued to celebrate Jewish holy days. On those days he fasted, asking the guard to give his small portion of food to his cellmates. Eventually, long nights of interrogation began, with prisoners summoned only by the first letter of their last names. The guards never called the full names aloud, as they did not want other prisoners to recognize those taken from their cells. Although he knew it would do him no good, Begin argued Herzl's vision of a united Jewish Israel. He explained Zionism and discussed Jabotinsky with his interrogators, using broken Russian. He discussed these topics only to strengthen his own determination to survive and return to his wife.

That reunion would not take place for years. Begin considered writing a document allowing Aliza an unconditional divorce. He might remain in prison for some time, and she should not suffer for something she could not control. As 1941 arrived, Begin and his cellmates continued to survive on a single meal each day. They learned to divide the tiny portion into even smaller servings so they might nibble throughout the day. A few days after the New Year, a guard transferred Begin into a larger communal cell of sixty prisoners, designed to hold only sixteen beds. He never saw his roommates again.

In his new surroundings, Begin learned to use taps on the wall to communicate with others. He also participated in a hunger strike, which succeeded in improving the prisoners' diet. Prison supervisors added cabbage soup two days each week and cereal soup five days per week. The prisoners celebrated that small victory. After speaking with a friend regarding his plans to divorce Aliza, he decided against it. The two agreed that sending such a document to their wives would only encourage their grief over the separation. That decision also made Begin feel more positive about his future.

Begin's victorious feelings did not last long. He suffered through a mock trial in April of 1941. As a result of his conviction, he received an eight-year sentence in a Russian labor camp in the frigid northern region known as Siberia. Ironically, the police based his sentence on an accusation that Begin served as a British spy, supporting the very nation, Great Britain, that Begin considered an oppressor of the Jewish state. One occurrence lifted his spirits somewhat. He found in a packet sent from Aliza a handkerchief with the letters "OLA" embroidered on it. At first puzzled, Begin could not understand why she might have altered her initials. Then a friend solved the riddle for him. They needed to read the initials as the word "Ola," in Hebrew the feminine word for "going to (settle in) the land of Israel." Unable to help her husband, Aliza had decided to go to Palestine, keeping faith that he would eventually join her.

Before leaving for Siberia, Begin heard rumors about prison camp life. Some held that life there was much preferable to life in the jail. Food would be more plentiful, and each man could work, rather than remaining confined to a cell. Not only that, prisoners would receive a small amount of pay for that work. He also learned that family could visit him in May, before his departure. He sent word to his home, and on the appointed day, a young woman named Paula, who he knew slightly from Betar, arrived. As she pretended to be Aliza, Begin understood that Aliza had already departed. He exchanged words in code with Paula and learned that his father and siblings were also safe, for the time being. Although the guards would not permit Paula to leave the food she had brought, they did hand over some small bars of soap to Begin. In one bar, Paula had concealed a note that confirmed the coded messages. Begin admired Paula's courage in impersonating his wife and hoped to thank her when he left prison. He learned much later that she died fighting the Germans.

As the freight train full of prisoners traveled to Siberia, Begin heard another rumor that some type of Soviet-Polish

Many Jews, including members of Begin's family, did not survive the deplorable conditions of the concentration camps. Even if they were not murdered in the gas chambers or ovens, starvation and diseases like typhus claimed many lives.

agreement was under discussion. He lost count of the number of days they traveled, as a weak sun seemed to shine constantly. Finally, a guard explained to the prisoners that they had traveled far enough north to reach the country of "white nights." The northern lights lit up the sky during what should have been dark hours.

Many prisoners became ill from the constant rocking of the train cars. After arriving at camp, they experienced endless attacks by bugs that lived in the sawdust of their bedding. They were told they should be grateful to be in camp, far from the "German cannibals." They learned they would be working on a railroad.

While the prisoners did receive measly wages for their efforts, they immediately spent them on whatever their captors would offer. After waiting in a long line they thought would lead to food, prisoners might discover instead the line "authorized" them to buy disinfectant. They had to pay for various "authorizations," often never receiving the promised item.

Begin heard a number of times from guards, "People don't get out of here. . . . you will not see the Jewish State." Fortunately, time proved them wrong. The pact between Russia and Poland that Begin had heard about became reality in 1941. He was one of 1.5 million Poles freed by Russia, due to their Polish citizenship.

After leaving Siberia, Begin launched a search for his family. Only his sister, Rachael, had survived the German prison camps. This made him more determined than ever to reach Palestine and campaign for a united state of Israel. He used his newly acquired English language skills, developed by listening to British radio broadcasts, to become an interpreter for the Polish Army. The army traveled first to Iran, then to Palestine.

Begin found Aliza and served as an army interpreter until December of 1943. During those early years in Palestine, he put the plans of his youth into motion. That feat proved a challenge, because Begin's ideas regarding a unified Israel contrasted sharply with those of Jewish Palestine's favorite political leader, David Ben-Gurion. A Polish-born Jew like Begin, Ben-Gurion had lived in Palestine for decades. He worked tirelessly to support Zionism, at first for the British who continued with a mandate, or permission, from the United Nations (UN) to keep order in Palestine. However, when the British greatly diminished the number of Jewish immigrants allowed to enter Palestine in 1929, Ben-Gurion split away. He then served as secretary for an organization of Jewish workers. Most of his followers were members of the Histadrut, or General Federation of Labor. In 1930, he formed the Zionist political Labor party, Mapai, and by 1935 chaired the executive committee of the Jewish Agency for Palestine. By 1939, over 100,000 additional Jews had migrated to Palestine, and Ben-Gurion, whose surname meant "son of a young lion," pushed even harder for organization.

Other political movements also gained strength. Ze'ev Jabotinsky, Begin's mentor, criticized Ben-Gurion's creation of a working-class movement. He felt it distracted Zionists from the true issue of statehood. That Begin would side with the philosophy of Jabotinsky upon his arrival in Palestine was hardly surprising. By 1943, Begin had a new reason to pursue statehood for Israel. His son, Benjamin Ze'ev (named for his father) was born. Benjamin would be followed by two daughters, Hasia, born in 1946 and named for his mother, and Leah, born in 1949. Throughout his life, Begin's family remained of crucial importance, and his devotion to Aliza became legendary. He saw his family's fate as being tied to Israel's fate. Begin transmitted his feelings so clearly to his family, that as an adult, Benjamin "Benji" Begin followed his father into a political career.

During the years that Ben-Gurion pursued independence through politics, Begin adopted a more active approach. He revitalized the Irgun Tzeva'I Le'umi, an underground military group. Called Irgun for short, the group was also known as ETZEL, a term that was a Hebrew acronym for "National Military Organization." Begin's bitter experiences with the Holocaust led to his support of the philosophy of revolution taught by Jabotinsky. He wrote that, "From my early youth, I had been taught by my father, who went to his death at Nazi hands voicing his faith in God and singing 'Hatikvah,' that we Jews were to return to the land of Israel—not go, travel or come, but return." In other words, Palestine represented land that belonged originally to the Jews. Any group who disagreed represented an enemy. Begin had an activist attitude, and through Etzel, he instituted what he considered acts of war. Others, however, termed his actions terrorism.

British and Arab forces both became Etzel's targets.

One of Etzel's most infamous acts was a 1946 bombing of a wing of the King David Hotel in Jerusalem. Etzel chose that target, because it housed offices of the British government, which continued to resist the push for a state of Israel. The bombing resulted in 100 deaths, including not only British officials, but also Jewish and Arab employees. An initial reward of $8,000 would be increased to $50,000 for the capture of Begin, who British authorities described as "grim-faced" and "bespectacled." Begin later wrote that the Etzel, or Irgun, responded with terrorism "in order to secure the annulment of a death 'sentence,' the arrest of more officers which did not prevent the murder of our captive comrades, the whipping of officers in retaliation for the whipping of our young solders, hangings in retaliation for hangings." He thus justified the hanging of three British army sergeants in retaliation for the British execution of captured Zionist fighters.

By 1947, the British were spending enormous amounts of money to support 100,000 troops in a peacekeeping effort between Arabs and Jews in Palestine. They decided to present the problem to the United Nations, which established a special session to study Palestine. Both the United States and the Soviet Union supported a plan for separation of Palestine into Arab and Jewish states. However, the League of Arab States Council in December 1947 declared it would block the resolution. U.S. President Truman at first reversed his support of the partition plan. When the Jews received military support from Czechoslovakia, they gained enough power to begin to unite the areas of Palestine designated to become Israeli states by the U.N. Shortly thereafter, President Truman decided to support a Jewish state.

In April of 1948, Etzel attacked an Arab village, Deir Yassin, killing more than 200 men, women, and children. The Palestinian Arab community reacted by fleeing areas

Israeli Prime Minister David Ben-Gurion signed a document on May 14, 1948 proclaiming the new Jewish State of Israel. Fifty-three nations, including Great Britain and Russia, recognized Israel's statehood, and the U.N. admitted Israel as a member in 1949.

with large Jewish populations. On May 14, 1948, Ben-Gurion proclaimed a state of Israel. On the following day, Britain gave up the U.N. mandate and departed the area, and the United States announced its recognition of Israel. By May 18, the Soviet Union recognized Israel, and by April of 1949, fifty-three nations, including Great Britain, did the same. In May of 1949, the United Nations admitted the nation of Israel as a member.

Shortly after the founding of statehood under the leadership of Ben-Gurion as prime minister, the vast differences between Ben-Gurion and Begin became more than just theory. Ben-Gurion believed that due to its small size, Israel as a Jewish state had to adhere to policies of stronger more powerful groups, such as the United States and the United Nations. In his opinion, Jewish unity problems began in ancient times with the Jewish resistance of the power of the Romans. That resistance brought about the disintegration of ancient Israel, an act repeated over history by Israel's lack of compliance with a long list of outside powers. This resistance had caused the failures of the Jewish people. By contrast, Begin believed that the major reason for the collapse was civil war among the Jews, an internal disagreement. He remained first a Jew, and second an Israeli. Such differences proved crucial to both men and to the history of Israel.

On May 28, 1948, Ben-Gurion unified Israel's military forces into one structure, the Israel Defense Forces (IDF). The Irgun challenged that formation, sailing the *Altalena*, an armed ship, into Tel Aviv harbor. In June, Ben-Gurion fired on the *Altalena*. He knew the ship brought arms for Israel, and that he fired on his own people. He did so because the ship's action of bearing arms directly contradicted an order of peace handed down by the U.N., an order that Ben-Gurion intended to support. Before all-out civil war could begin, Menachem Begin boarded the ship and ordered it not to return fire. Historians claim this as one of the greatest moments of Begin's life. Ben-Gurion's belief in conforming to a stronger power guided his actions, while Begin's adamant stand against Jews fighting Jews guided his. The face-off brought to a close Begin's career as leader of Irgun, which was dissolved. He converted his armed movement into a political party called the Herut, or Freedom Movement.

To the world outside of Israel, Irgun's attacks against Arabs and the British remained incomprehensible. To many,

Begin's reputation as a bloodthirsty terrorist would stay with him forever. However, for others, he was a freedom fighter, who, before the creation of the state of Israel, brought equality and unity to Palestine's various Jewish communities. Seen by many as "a bridge-builder," Begin often declared, " 'Yehudim Anakhnu!' ('We are the Jews!') [and] he meant it." He refused to view his people in any other way. This vision of a united Israel would one day catapult him into the highest office in the land.

Begin casts his vote in the 1949 elections to Israel's Knesset, or parliament. Ben-Gurion's Labor party won a majority of the seats, while Begin's Herut party took only 14.

3

The Power
of the Party

A lthough Israel had ended fighting among its own people, it still faced all the challenges expected of a brand new government. Prime Minister Ben-Gurion dealt with several different political parties, one of which was Begin's newly organized Herut, or Freedom Movement. A temporary group called the Provisional Council of State immediately ended all restriction on Jewish immigration into Israel. Ben-Gurion made sure to retain control during the transition period. A constitution that the new Constituent Assembly was to write by October 1948 did not materialize.

However, on February 16, 1949, the Constituent Assembly converted into Israel's Knesset, or parliament. It acted as Israel's house of representatives. Israel settled upon a democratic system containing a separation of powers into three groups, the legislative, the executive and the judiciary. The Knesset was the legislative branch with 120 members, elected every four years. It passed "basic laws" on which the new government would be based.

In the January 1949 elections to the Knesset, Ben-Gurion's Labor party, the Mapai, took 44 seats for its representatives. A more liberal group called Mapam won 15 seats, a religious group took 16, and Begin's Herut party claimed only 14. While Ben-Gurion placed Chaim Weizmann, a cultural Zionist, at the Knesset's head as president, clearly that position carried little power. Israel's president would forever act only as a figurehead, elected every five years by the Knesset. Whichever political party had the most seats in the Knesset, and therefore the most power, would choose their own representative as president. Then the president formally appointed the leader of the party with the most seats to become prime minister. The prime minister then selected up to 18 other ministers, half of whom had to serve in the Knesset. That group became his cabinet; it would run the government.

Begin's party elected him to the Knesset as a conservative. Despite some dissension in Herut, Begin retained the pro-Jabotinsky stance. He managed to convince his opponents of his worth as a leader. He trusted a small group of aides that included, among others, Chaim Landau and Yohanan Bader, from whom he demanded complete loyalty. He rarely sought their advice and became known as an autocrat, a leader who retained total power. Many intellectuals left Herut, due to Begin's non-democratic style.

The Herut stood in direct opposition to Ben-Gurion's liberal party, the Mapai. The Mapai supported the mostly concrete and specific needs of a select group, Israel's working class. The Herut, however, established itself as a party of all Israeli citizens. It based its platform on a romantic nationalistic approach. The Herut made clear its mission to restore Israel to its ancient glory and to use military force to do so. Begin's supporters declared him the only man who could help reach that dream, based on his history as a freedom fighter. The

Many Arabs, like these Arab refugees fleeing Palestine in 1948, were driven from their homeland when Jewish immigrants claimed their land for Israel. Begin was anti-Arab, and encouraged Jews to retaliate against Arab freedom fighters.

enmity between the two leaders remained fierce. Ben-Gurion and Begin often sat only feet from one another, taking tea in the Knesset dining room. Still, the Prime Minister refused to speak Begin's name. Instead, during debates in Knesset, Ben-Gurion referred to his younger opponent as "that man sitting next to Member of Knesset Bader."

Disputes over Arab control of territory concerned all political parties. Palestinian Arab refugees claimed the Jews had driven them from their homeland; they wanted to return as Arabs. Before 1949, about 1.3 million Arabs lived in what would become Israel; after 1949, that number had shrunk to about 170,000. Those remaining inside the new State of Israel automatically became citizens with voting rights. According to

Israel's Declaration of Independence, Arab citizens would enjoy social and political equality with Jewish citizens. However, because an Israeli Constitution never passed, those promised rights remained threatened. All circumstances after the formation of the state encouraged the development of Jewish institutions, many of which infringed on Arab rights. Jewish Immigrants could claim Arab land, the Hebrew language dominated Arabic, and Judaism dominated Islam. Arab groups received little government assistance supporting their farms and businesses.

Begin remained anti-Arab. When Arab freedom fighters struck, he urged that Israel retaliate in kind. He also blocked relationships with England, which he believed to be pro-Nazi, and West Germany, declaring "every German a Nazi, every German a murderer." Begin's loss of many family members to the Nazis, along with his imprisonment, proved crucial to forming his life-long opinions. At one point, the Knesset suspended Begin for organizing protests.

Still, Begin did not resemble a revolutionary, but then he never had. Even during his activities with Etzel after 1943, he had led a regular daily routine as a husband and father to Benjamin, Hasia, and Leah. He enjoyed reading the Palestinian Jewish press. He also continued listening to the BBC and reading British papers to improve his English. Begin did have a special hiding place in the attic of his apartment house, which he had used for three days following the bombing of the King David Hotel. Throughout his career, he always dressed in a conservative suit and tie. Unlike his fellow Knesset members who arrived to the group's first meeting in limousines, Begin walked from his apartment.

Herut could not make much headway in the Knesset, due to Ben-Gurion's ignoring of Begin. In his writings, Ben-Gurion represented himself as a biblical scholar and historian. Begin took a different approach, emphasizing his knowledge of law and its formal language, Latin. Many observers felt Begin's approach to be too formal and repetitive, but he kept that style throughout his tenure in government. He would remain in the shadow of Ben-Gurion, who hoped to destroy the socialist Zionism that Begin represented. In Ben-Gurion's opinion, that movement was too romantic and depended too much on militarism.

Begin's strict control within his party prevented any real leadership from developing to push the Mapai from power. If anyone from within his own party tried to introduce new ideas that challenged Begin, they would also be challenging Herut's goal of one Israel. Begin continued his struggle to transform himself from a militant to a politician. At the same time, Ben-Gurion retained his long-time stance as an Israel insider. Filled with contempt for the "newcomer," Ben-Gurion never hid his feelings. He publicly labeled Begin a "bespectacled petty Polish solicitor" and even a "clown."

In an attempt to settle some of the land squabbles between Israel and its neighbors, Ben-Gurion approved a treaty draft in February 1950. King Abdullah of Transjordan, later to become Jordan, signed the treaty. Transjordan had previously been occupied by Arabs. In April, the king took over the West Bank and East Jerusalem. Bounded on the south, north, and west by Israel, the West Bank butted up against Transjordan on its east side. It remained important to Israel's security. In addition, Jerusalem was the most important holy city to the Jews. Thus, King Abdullah's claims infuriated many Israelis.

Ben-Gurion complied with King Abdullah's wishes, because he believed that would end all Arab claims on Israeli land. However, in July of 1951, Abdullah was assassinated, and all of Israel's Arab neighbors boycotted the country. Israel lost the use of the important Suez Canal and the Strait of Tiran. Ben-Gurion attempted to form a "new guard" in the Mapai by introducing the war hero, General Moshe Dayan, and the politician, Shimon Peres. Throughout the 1950s, this new guard would compete with the original members of Mapai for power. Just as in Begin's Herut party, internal conflict plagued the Mapai.

In November 1953, Ben-Gurion resigned and the militaristic Moshe Sharett replaced him. Under Sharett's weak leadership, a major scandal occurred in the Mapai when Israeli spies were caught and executed in Egypt. In February of 1955, Ben-Gurion returned to the Ministry of Defense, and attacks against Egypt continued. Concerned with the rise in power of the Egyptian leader Gamal Abdul Nasser, the Mapai returned Ben-Gurion to the post of Prime Minister.

Following Ben-Gurion's return, a famous debate took place between him and Begin in 1955. Begin was still arguing that Etzel had broken no laws and had not urged civil war when it operated in the 1940s. He referred to the *Altalena* incident when he pointed at Ben-Gurion and declared, "He had ordered to shoot at me with a cannon." Ben-Gurion agreed without hesitation, "I was the man who issued the order for a holy cannon to fire on the ship." He continued, "We voted to destroy the *Altalena* and our decision came to fruition." Begin replied, "The words, the deed, is that you spilled innocent blood." Such exchanges were frequent. However, Ben-Gurion had more serious concerns.

The Israeli Ministry of Defense had power over three areas of land, all constantly threatened by various Arab countries surrounding Israel. The Northern area, known as Little Galilee, held about 66% of Israel's Arab population. A second small piece of land called the "Little Triangle" lay between two villages, Et Tira and Et Taiyiba, located close to Israel's border with Transjordan. Finally, the Negev Desert made up most of the third area. Populated mostly by non-political Bedouins constantly on the move to support their families, it held the least threat to Israeli control. Egyptian forces wanted control of Transjordan, and Ben-Gurion had a conflict to face.

By October of 1956, Egypt's President Nasser could buy arms from the Soviet Union and Czechoslovakia. At the same time, U.S. President Dwight D. Eisenhower refused to send Israel any weapons. Ben-Gurion talked secretly with France and Britain about an Israeli military strike on the Sinai, which those countries would support. They worked together to chase the Egyptian Army from the Suez. Soon after their victory, the Europeans agreed to a cease-fire following pressure by Eisenhower who feared the Soviets, a growing threat to the U.S., might become involved. Although the Israelis left the Sinai in 1957, Ben-Gurion declared the war a success. Arab raids from Gaza, a crucial area south of Egypt, ceased. United Nations peacekeepers separated Egypt from Israel. In addition, arms sales to Israel from France increased and, with France's help, Israel constructed a nuclear reactor to produce badly needed power.

Equally important to Ben-Gurion was the fact that his new military organization, the Israel Defense Forces (IDF), had proven its worth. It would rapidly gain a well-deserved reputation as one of the best fighting forces in the world. Service in the IDF was required of all eighteen-year old citizens, both male and female, as well as of aliens who lived in Israel long term. Rules regarding the length of time served changed over time, but an average for males was three years compared to twenty months for females. Some exemptions, or releases from military service, were available, but not usually to males. The IDF drafted about 90 percent of eighteen-year old males each year, amounting annually to approximately 30,000 new service men. Students could go into a military "reserve," gaining their bachelor's degree before service. The IDF boasted several "elite," or highly expert, units composed completely of volunteers. The air force received first choice of the most outstanding candidates. Despite all of Ben-Gurion's criticism of Begin's Herut party for being militaristic, he remained fully aware of the importance of a sharp military force.

All Israeli citizens, both male and female, serve in the Israeli Defense Forces (IDF). These female Israeli soldiers pose in the Sinai Dessert after Israel's victory over Egypt in 1956.

The war and the IDF development caused an effect that Ben-Gurion did not anticipate. It actually changed public opinion toward Herut, now the country's second strongest political party. Herut's image suddenly seemed less militant in the wake of the Mapai-led military assaults. In addition, its opposition to the withdrawal from Sinai drew no criticism. Thus, Israel's shaky relationship with Egypt became a crucial aspect of Begin's political life.

Begin continued to struggle, along with his party, for a stronger voice in government. He complained that he received more respect when he traveled abroad than in Israel. When he visited Argentina, he found its president, Juan Peron, warm and accepting. In New York City, people treated him as a celebrity. He would at last receive stronger support in Israel in the later 1950s, when Jewish immigrants greatly increased the new state's population. That group saw themselves in the Polish-born Begin who was, like them, an outsider.

In 1956, Begin began to search for another group to strengthen the voice of Herut. He tried at several conventions over the years to join with the Liberal party and form a coalition. His proposal was defeated in the fifth Herut conference in 1958, but it gained attention. In 1963, Ben-Gurion resigned from his party due to a dispute. He helped form the Rafi party with Moshe Dayan and Shimon Peres, but by 1967, would no longer be involved in politics. Those developments opened the door for Begin to step into the power he had long desired.

In Herut's seventh conference in 1964, Begin again pushed to negotiate a coalition, or joint power. Changing circumstances inside the Liberal party made it ripe for such a union, and a new conservative party emerged in 1965. Called the Gahal, it was composed of the Herut and the Liberal party. In the 1966 elections, Gahal gained a total of 26 seats, not a tremendous number, but still a challenge to the Mapai.

During the sixties, Begin spent most of his time in Tel Aviv, either at Herut headquarters, nicknamed Jabotinsky's Castle, or at his home, a three-room apartment on the ground floor of a condominium at No. 1 Rosenbaum Street. He lived a routine existence, often inviting friends and supporters for weekend visits in a warm and comfortable atmosphere.

Menachem and Aliza Begin generally began entertaining on Saturdays, after 5:00 P.M., the official end of the Sabbath. On those occasions, visitors would see a more relaxed, informal Begin. Without his trademark suit and tie, sometimes even unshaven, he greeted guests with hugs, often kissing their hands. Favorite phrases of Begin, "We are all simple men and women" and "simple Jews" also greeted his visitors.

In 1966, Begin faced a challenge from within the ranks of the new party by a man named Shmuel Tamir. Tamir had challenged Begin once before, and he insisted both times that Herut needed to find an alternative to what he saw as Begin's "petrified ideology." He wanted Herut to come to an agreement with the National Workers Union, a labor group traditionally supported by the Mapai. They were also supported by the General Zionists, a group that shared Begin's image of a united Israel. Begin had also seen the potential in gaining the Union's support. He developed a "Blue-and-White" plan that would allow the Union and the General Zionists to combine forces with Herut. His plan narrowly passed, and he once again remained the head of his political party. Within months, he would announce a dramatic resignation, saying "I am returning my Knesset membership to the movement that elected me." In reality, his resignation was only to attract attention, and Begin never left his chairmanship of Herut. Supporters developed slogans, like "Begin, Begin, the power must stay with Begin, . . . He saved the nation from a holocaust: he transfused the nation with pride. Without Begin we would go to our grave."

In 1967 an event took place that transformed all of Israel and also Begin's position within his country's government. Israel's Arab neighbors, Egypt, Syria and Jordan, attacked Israel. Israel then retaliated. Labeled The Six-Day War, the fight ended Egypt's power over the Arab world and altered the shape of Israel. It offered Begin a new role within Herut as the party saw the achievement of Eretz Israel within its grasp.

Between May 15 and June 2, 1967, Israel had engaged in one of its strongest diplomatic conflicts. Levi Eshkol, the Mapai Prime Minister and Defense Minister, along with the IDF Chief of Staff, Yitzhak Rabin, learned that Nasser had proclaimed a state of emergency in Egypt. He ousted U.N. forces from the

Egypt, Syria, and Jordan attacked Israel in 1967, setting off the Six-Day War. Well-trained Israeli soldiers were victorious over their Arab enemies, and Israel quadrupled the area of land it controlled.

Sinai and closed the Straits of Aqaba, important waterways for trade with Israel. Clearly, Egypt challenged Israel to strike back. He decided to consult with his advisors, the IDF and important national leaders as to whether to go to war. Eshkol lacked the respect and leadership qualities of David Ben-Gurion. Within days, a new unified, or coalition, national government would emerge. Not trusting Eshkol to represent the country, leaders from all political parties decided to take control together.

Much turmoil preceded the forming of the coalition. In addition to Begin, figures involved included Begin's supporters Arieh Ben Eliezer and Chaim Landau, and Fafi members Peres and Yoseh Almogi, formerly of the Mapai. As the men gathered to consult with Eshkol, a clever Begin stunned his one-time rival, Peres. He asked whether Ben-Gurion could return to resume power over a new national unity government. Near age eighty, Ben-Gurion had declared permanent retirement from politics, a fact that both Begin and Peres knew. However, simply by his suggestion, Begin set the stage for the development of a new partnership between former enemies. Remarkably, Ben-Gurion would agree to return to government. Begin, caught up in the role of publicly supporting a man that Israel's population revered, agreed to help him. Begin helped convince Ben-Gurion to return as prime minister with Eshkol as his deputy.

Many members of the Knesset opposed Ben-Gurion's return. However, they liked the idea of a national unity government. Eshkol had unknowingly invited his long-time rivals to take part in a rare opportunity to remove him from power. No one had really taken seriously that Ben-Gurion would return, but now the way had opened for Moshe Dayan, who had Begin's support, to move into the cabinet as defense minister. Peres promoted Dayan's appointment, but others opposed it. One of those individuals, Knesset member Golda Meir, was a veteran of many political wars who would prove vital to Israel's future.

The IDF High Command became anxious as they watched the prospects for war increase. Diplomacy with Egypt on the part of the United States had not proven successful. The IDF prepared for war as Peres pressured Mapai leaders for a national unity government. The public supported the new government plan. Women demonstrated outside of Mapai headquarters, while Israeli newspapers screamed for a coalition.

On June 1, 1967, later to be called "The Longest Day," Begin's party, Gahal, pushed hard for unity. Leaders including Peres came to Begin's apartment, crowded with political figures, to urge him to support Dayan's appointment. Begin not only agreed to support his former opponent, he told Eshkol that without Dayan as national defense minister, there could be no national unity government. Despite the protests of Golda Meir and others, the national government was becoming a reality. Rabin, the chief-of-staff, stated that he did not care who headed the Defense Ministry, as long as a quick appointment could be made. Eshkol decided on Dayan, which signaled the beginning of the unity government.

Members of Herut appointed Begin their representative. On June 6, 1967, after twenty years struggling to become a political power, Menachem Begin joined a brand new coalition government. He assumed a position labeled Minister Without Portfolio, meaning without a specific area of government to control; he would hold that title for three years. At 5 A.M. on June 6, the Israeli Air Force effectively destroyed the ground forces of its Arab enemies. It then took control over an area approximately four times its own size. That catapulted Moshe Dayan into the press. A distinctive black patch covered a 1941 wound that had resulted in the loss of his eye. It served to enhance his warrior image. Suddenly, Dayan became the most photographed political figure of his age.

The war created new leaders, in both a military and a political sense. Begin saw the possibilities. By aligning himself with powerful political heroes who had once been his enemies, Menachem Begin had assured his future in the government of Israel.

Begin poses with General Ariel Sharon on the Southern Front of the Six-Day War. Throughout his career, Begin would defend Israel's right to maintain a presence in former Arab territories and refused to discuss any retreat from these areas until a peace treaty was in place.

4

A New
Prime Minister:
A Renewed Vision

In his new position as a minister, Begin pressured Eshkol's administration to enter the war with force. He encouraged the capture of the sacred city of Jerusalem. He also believed that Israel should control a 480 square mile area known as the Golan Heights. Located in Southwestern Syria, the Golan Heights was named for its hills overlooking Syria's capital city of Damascus and the Syrian plains. It would provide Israel with a military advantage in the case of attack.

For the next three years, Begin served on various committees, always protesting any talk of retreat from land desired by the Arabs without a full peace treaty. Among his proposals was the establishment of Jewish quarters in Arab cities in what others termed "occupied territories," meaning that Israelis occupied foreign land. Begin never liked that phrase. Decades later following his election as prime minister, he visited a settlement of Jews in the West Bank, an area of approximately 2200 square miles. Begin corrected reporters who used the West Bank name, telling them to call the territory by its biblical names, Judea and Samaria. He preferred the term "liberated territories" to the term "occupied." When the reporters asked whether the areas would be "annexed," taken into Israel, Begin explained, "You annex foreign land, not your own country." Begin felt that Jews living in such areas would add stability and create trust with the Arabs, even though others argued their presence simply increased tensions.

Another political change occurred when Prime Minister Eshkol died on February 26, 1969. Golda Meir took over as Labor Party leader and then prime minister. She stood as strongly against the Arabs as Begin, and he supported her. However, he still worked to eventually gain the power that he saw her hold. In 1970 when President Nasser of Egypt died, he was replaced by Anwar Sadat. Almost immediately, Sadat attempted to gain access to the Sinai through negotiations.

Begin protested a 1970 peace plan suggested by U.S. Secretary of State William Rogers that would not allow Israel's direct negotiation with the Arabs. Begin believed the plan would allow the Egyptians to launch a full attack against Israel. Referring to a once Nazi-occupied German city, Begin labeled the plan a "Middle Eastern Munich." He, along with five Gahal ministers, resigned when the coalition voted to accept the Rogers Plan.

Soon after a cease-fire between Israel and Egypt took effect, Begin found another opportunity to criticize the Meir government. The Egyptians immediately established a new missile base close to the line of cease-fire. He began to build support for a new political party. Gahal became more popular when General Ariel Sharon joined. Having gained fame as a fighter, he had long been a public favorite. Soon members of other parties followed Sharon. The group formed the Likud Block, with Begin as leader.

Despite Israel's constant focus on its Arab neighbors, those neighbors managed to catch it off guard. Egypt and Syria together attacked Israel on October 6, 1973 in an offensive that

Golda Meir was blamed for Israel's poor performance in the Yom Kippur War of 1973; she resigned as prime minister shortly after. Begin's popularity increased during this period, making him a strong candidate for prime minister in 1977.

would be called the Yom Kippur War. Named for the Jewish religious celebration of forgiveness held annually at the end of September or beginning of October, the war took Israel by surprise. Most Israeli Jews were fasting or praying, observing Yom Kippur rituals, when Syria, aided by Jordan and Iraq, attacked the Golan Heights. At the same time, Egypt entered a part of the Sinai occupied by Israel. On October 16, the Israelis counterattacked by entering Egypt. By October 22, the U.N. had negotiated a cease-fire. Golda Meir received the blame for Israel's lack of preparedness, and protestors marched outside her office demanding her resignation. When she resigned the following June, Begin's voice was one of the loudest calling for her removal. He also criticized the United States for giving in to the Arabs. The Yom Kippur War marked the first instance in which the Arabs used oil as a bargaining tool. They threatened not to sell oil to any countries that supported Israel.

Along with Meir, Moshe Dayan, once a major war hero, lost his popularity. In the public's eyes, Dayan failed at his post of defense minister by not remaining alert to attack. When Golda Meir retired in 1964, Dayan accompanied her. Yom Kippur was a war fought by junior officers in which more than 3000 Israelis had died. The public long remembered the lack of leadership by Meir and her cabinet. When she left office, her party appointed Yitzhak Rabin to replace her. Rabin became the first native-born Israeli to hold the office of prime minister.

In all of the turmoil, Begin never once changed his long-time attitude. He constantly stressed Israel's claim to the West Bank as originally a part of ancient Israel. He argued it proved crucial to the security of Israel in protecting itself from invasion. Threats of such invasion continued to grow, due to the growing activity of the Palestinian Liberation Organization (PLO). When U.S. Secretary of State Henry Kissinger suggested that Israel "trade territory for legitimacy," Begin retorted, "We exist. Therefore we are legitimate."

As the election of 1977 approached, onlookers had to agree that Begin was a strong candidate for prime minister. Since 1948, he had demonstrated many desirable leadership qualities, including great rhetorical skills and charisma. As a traditional Jew, he continued to appeal to many staunch followers of Judaism. However, he also had an obvious weakness. He had for years attacked the Labor party for supporting socialism, a governing approach in which the government would control production of goods and the distribution of its country's wealth. Yet, Begin had never developed a clear program against social-ism. Domestic concerns, such as the provision of enough jobs for all Israelites, high wages and support for farms and business, had always been less important to Begin. He focused on fighting the Arab countries and the achievement of Eretz Israel. In addition, his own political party often exhibited a lack of unity.

To accommodate his critics, Begin softened his public words and sharpened his great skills as a campaigner. Still, he did not change his attitudes. He told one official, "I am willing to learn history from you up the First World War. However, with regards to what happened subsequently, I don't learn history from anybody." His Likud Party became known as the party of the homeless and the poor. He disagreed with the acceptance of money from Germany, which sought to pay its debts to the Jews who had suffered and died during the World War II. Rabin waved away Begin's comments as the grumbling of an old-timer, calling him a piece from a museum. According to Rabin, Begin's time had passed.

Rabin himself, however, did not prove a successful leader. Shy and nervous, he was not the right person to restore respect for the government to the people of Israel. During a huge 1977 celebration of the victory of Israel's basketball team over Russia's team, Rabin appeared on television to make an announcement. He and his family had been accused of holding an illegal American bank account. The Labor Zionist's reputation for honesty and ethics continued to unravel, and Rabin resigned his party's leadership position. In his place, Shimon Peres would represent Labor in the upcoming elections.

Then Begin suffered a massive heart attack. While he recovered, long-time party member Ezer Weizman took over, and many observers believed that Weizman would run against Peres. Weizman had a reputation for a ripe sense of humor. He often exchanged jokes at stoplights, beckoning to people in cars beside him to roll down their windows. He also had been known to hide in the bushes and jump out to scare his friends. His approach contrasted greatly with Begin's sober one. A military hero for his actions while Air Force Chief during the 1967 war, Weizman was also the nephew of Chaim Weizman, the country's first president. He could prove to be an agreeable candidate. Weizman also had a history of contesting Begin; in 1970, he had attempted to assume control of the party. The Israeli public felt the possibility for change that the May 17 election represented, and for the first time in years, emotions over the elections ran high.

Many in the Likud Party felt Begin was too old, after a thirty-year career, to become Prime Minister. They also disliked his controlling approach; only he determined the party ideals and goals. For this very reason, his effect on party members was strong. One younger member once joked during a meeting, "When I was a little kid, my mother used to warn me that if I didn't finish my supper, Begin would come and get me." As those present at the meeting laughed, he remained serious, adding, "you don't forget something like that." Those who had known of Begin for years remembered the days that this seemingly calm man had been classified a terrorist and a Public Enemy by the British. Weizman, though, decided to continue his support for Begin. He told other party members that he would not contest Begin as the Likud's candidate.

Begin's illness actually proved positive to the campaign. The opposition certainly could not make fun of a sick man, perhaps close to death. Previously, they willingly made known their opinions of Begin as a clown. Now, when the public viewed him as a brave campaigner, they had to remain silent.

When Begin left the hospital to appear on television during the end of the campaign, he refused to wear make-up or the blue shirt that his advisors requested. Dressed in a bright white shirt and tie, he appeared weak, but remained as idealistic as ever. He still described himself simply as an "Old Jew." He had a new enemy to verbally attack—the PLO. He labeled its members "Arab Nazis" in his article, "Arab Nazism Against the Jewish Boy." The article referred to the Ma'alot massacre in which PLO members captured a school bus that was later stormed by the IDF. Several Israeli children died in the confrontation. He wrote that Israel needed to fight harder than even to combat "Arab Nazism," emphasizing the powerful state Israel had become. He added that if Jews had had that kind of power before World War II, "we could have hit hard at Hitler, Himmler, Eichmann," and "relentlessly hit them."

Menachem Begin celebrates on May 17, 1977 as he hears the announcement of his election as the sixth prime minister of Israel.

Shortly before midnight on May 17, 1977, news announcers delivered the astonishing news. Ben-Gurion's Mapai, the Labor Party, had at last been defeated. Menachem Begin was Israel's sixth prime minister, and the Likud the party in power. The results stunned everyone, including so-called political experts. At headquarters, Begin's supporters shouted and pounded one another on the back. Tears ran down the cheeks of the long-time Herut members. They had waited thirty long years for this victory.

Some members of Labor proved to be sore losers, labeling Begin's victory a mistake due to faulty vote counting. Many in the Labor party considered the Likud a bunch of "pioneers" who had rejected valuable socialist ideas to chase a vision. The Likud members were not Israelis, they were "just Jews." But Begin ignored such opinions. The day following the election he visited a West Bank settlement and declared, "We stand on the land of liberated Israel . . . there will be many, many settlements in the coming weeks."

Menachem Begin had lost eight elections in a row, but his confidence had not been broken. His favorite saying, "by the ballot, not the bullet," had come to pass. If surprised by his win, he did not show it. He had waited a long time to assume leadership of his country, and his plan was clear. Begin supported what seemed contradictory goals, to control territory desired by Israel's Arab enemies, but also to achieve peace with the Arabs. He had to work craftily to achieve his goal.

In his zeal to support Judaism, Begin made a well-meaning blunder during his early days in office. He wanted to select a Sephardic Jew as president. The Sephardic Jews claimed as their ancestors Spanish Jews who, in the fifteenth century, had left Spain due to persecution. They relocated to Africa and Asia, and claimed to be the original Jews, traditional heirs to Abraham's promise. Begin had somehow won over this sect of Israel's Jews, and they supported him in the election. They liked his fondness for tradition. It was obvious in his support of the right of Jews to retain their rituals, old-sounding names for their children, their special music and diet.

While the Sephardic Jews applauded Begin's decision to select one of their own for the symbolically important office of president, they did not support his specific choice. Because he knew of no Sephardic Jew qualified for the job, Begin asked for suggestions. To the puzzlement of many, he picked a little-known scientist, Itzhak Chavet, working at the Weizmann Institute for Science, named for Chaim Weizmann. Confused when asked to take the office, Chavet thought he was being offered the presidency of the Institute. Few members of Begin's own party, the Likud, agreed with Chavet's nomination. In the end, the Labor party's candidate, also a Sephardic named Yitzhak Navon, became president. For the first time, the party in power did not get to choose the president. Begin had suffered his first public political embarrassment.

Even though the Likud won the election, the Labor party still controlled much of the country's wealth and power. Begin needed to carefully establish a government that would allow him access to some of Labor's wealth. He decided to build some bridges with individuals from other parties. The Herut party lacked many members with administrative or political experience, mainly due to Begin's tight control. Weizman would be defense minister, Sharon minister of agriculture, and Simha Ehrlich, from the original Liberal party, minister of finance. Other cabinet members would have to come from other parties.

Within days of his election, however, Begin appeared to have another heart attack. While still in the hospital undergoing tests, he issued a surprise announcement. He wanted Moshe Dayan, Israel's one-time war hero, to serve as his foreign minister. Labor party members became upset, but Dayan welcomed the appointment. He had just been elected to the Knesset as a Labor member, but felt that he had been mistreated by his party in the past. Like Begin, he had been in and out of favor, and did not think that he owed his future to a bunch of politicians. When members of the Knesset filled out biography sheets before a session, Dayan had always listed his occupation only as "farmer." Close observers of the political scene should have been prepared for Begin's choice. He and Dayan had met together on many occasions to discuss Israel's future. On April 22, Begin had published an article titled, "Eretz Israel and Clarifications with Mr. Dayan." In the article, Begin clarified points on which he believed that he and Dayan agreed and disagreed. Although he denied rumors that his party wanted Dayan in its ranks, he clearly remained interested.

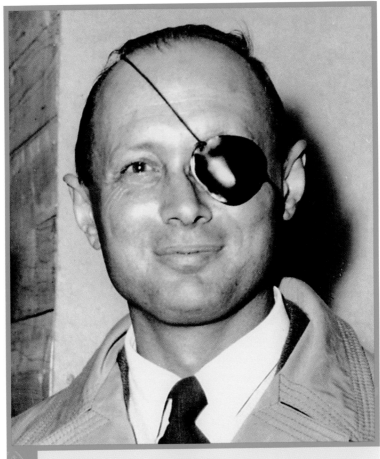

Begin admired General Moshe Dayan's political ideology as well as his public appeal, and appointed him Israel's foreign minister.

Begin did not care that Dayan had left his former appointment under Golda Meir in disgrace. He also ignored Dayan's reputation as a womanizer; the sister of his good friend Ezer Weizman had divorced Dayan. Begin valued Dayan's experience, and also the public's endless fascination with him. Others may have only seen irony in Begin's selection of a protégé of David Ben-Gurion, but Begin saw the selection as good politics. To him, Dayan represented a symbol of Eretz

Israel, born and raised on Israeli soil. Unfortunately, Dayan would prove more popular during Begin's early administration than Begin himself.

In addition to Dayan, Begin also wanted to bring another of Ben-Gurion's protégés, Professor Yigael Yadin, into his cabinet. A long-time archeologist, Yadin had reluctantly served Ben-Gurion in the military. Eventually, he abandoned that position to return to his major occupation. He had earned a Ph.D. from Harvard for his work on the famed Dead Sea Scrolls, a group of hundreds of ancient manuscripts discovered in a group of caves in Jordan. Highly regarded as an intellectual hero, Yadin remained popular with the public and politicians alike. When first asked by Begin to become Israel's Deputy Prime Minister, he declined. But eventually, convinced by his own Democratic Party for Change that he would overshadow Begin and take full control, Yadin agreed.

Begin would add, along with Dayan and Weizman, a third general to his cabinet, Ariel Sharon. Long known as a "hawk," one who supported war, he became Begin's minister of agriculture. While that may have seemed a strange title, in that position Sharon could prepare land for the Jewish settlements that Begin so strongly desired.

His powerful cabinet in place, Begin strongly emerged as prime minister. Much of the world did not know how to receive him. In Britain where he had once had a bounty on his head, Queen Elizabeth refused to see him for years. She would not formally receive "a former terrorist leader." His televised visit to the West Bank settlement of Elon Moreh following his election allowed viewers the world over to observe him dancing with the settlers, a Bible held high over his head. That action left no doubt that he would remain firmly committed to the religious goal of Eretz Israel. Within weeks, those who did not know of Begin would recognize his name. He began a historic move toward peace with Egypt that would confirm his place in history.

Begin made achieving peace with Egypt his priority. The new prime minister was very traditional, but also knew how to use the media to advance his causes. He is seen here in an television interview on "Face the Nation" in 1977, discussing the peace process.

5

Peace and Fame

Now that Begin had achieved his life-long dream of the leadership of Israel, he had other goals to reach. He wanted peace with at least a portion of his Arab neighbors. Peace would mean no more threats to the goal of Eretz Israel. In addition, peace would bring eternal fame and a place in history.

Begin's formal manner would result in a formal peace, the "old fashioned" type, with lots of meetings and ceremony. Always one who appreciated tradition, Begin could bring his traditional ways to the world through televised peace negotiations. Celebrations included parades and elaborate ceremonies to receive various delegations, or gatherings of diplomats.

Before he could begin serious work toward his goal of peace, Begin had to organize his cabinet. Made up of individuals from political parties including the old Herut, the Liberals, the

National Religious Party, and the Democratic Party for Change, cooperation proved essential. Working in Begin's favor was his autocratic, controlling approach. The Labor party, made up of union members who sometimes would not speak to one another outside of meetings, had been divisive. During their several decades of political power, their loud, disruptive arguments become legendary. That would not be true of the group controlled by Menachem Begin. For the first two years of his administration, Begin maintained strict authority.

Two major issues remained of highest priority for the cabinet: peace with Egypt and advancing Jewish settlements. Begin focused on the peacemaking and left settlement plans to Sharon, his aggressive minister of agriculture. With a reputation for activism, Sharon would work tirelessly to settle Judea and Samaria. His enthusiasm for his work resulted from boundless energy, an energy that matched his great appetite for food. He was a large man in every sense of the word. Sharon established settlements right next to Arab centers. He also developed a system of roads designed to isolate Israel's Arab population on the West Bank. The roads would also serve the military well, should they be needed. Radical groups, following Sharon's admired leadership, flocked to settle the areas. In a matter of years, the West Bank's Jewish population would double. Sharon's loyalty to Begin remained firm, as he hoped to one day take over Weizman's post as defense minister.

At the beginning of the administration, Weizman had little to do. However, he did control the occupied territories and could loudly express his opinion in the attitudes toward the Palestinians. He had selected a Sharon sympathizer, Rafael Eitan as his chief of staff of the IDF. He described Eitan as "a fighting horse," an excellent general who had no interest in politics.

As for Israel's foreign policy, the rational Dayan would help balance Begin's idealistic approach. Known as a pragmatist, Dayan historically chose logic over emotion when searching for solutions. Because they were each Zionists, they became an effective team. Both Begin and Dayan believed in direct negotiations. They did not care to use an intermediary, a representative from another country, as a go-between; Dayan once wrote an article titled "Negotiating Without Mediators." As for Begin, he had made clear his opinion about such intermediaries in his blasting of the 1969 Rogers Plan. Now in 1977, he again had to deal with what he saw as interference by the United States. He had watched as a U.S. mediator, Secretary of State Henry Kissinger, used "shuttle diplomacy" during the early 1970s. Kissinger flew back and forth between Israel and Egypt, and his efforts had resulted in a treaty of sorts. Now with the new U.S. President Jimmy Carter in power, attempts at diplomacy continued.

Both men also opposed the Palestinian plan to establish a West Bank independent state. Finally, they shared the opinion that Israel must keep security tight on the Jordan River. They did understand that in order to achieve a peace with Egypt, Israel would have to give up settlements in the Sinai. Dayan accepted that fact, even though as the former defense minister, he had helped initiate those settlements. While firm in his resolve to make Eretz Israel reality, Begin also desired that the world view him as just and fair. He wanted to show others that Israel anchored its civil system in democracy.

Soon after election, Begin made a move that his Labor predecessors would never have taken. On June 21, 1977, he publicly appealed to Israel's Arab neighbors in a speech to the Knesset. He addressed his appeal to King Hussein of Jordan, President Assad of Syria and President Sadat of Egypt, inviting them to meet him in either public or private. He called for an end to bloodshed, stating, "Too much Jewish and Arab blood has been shed in this region."

Begin did not delay in his push for a peace agreement with Egypt. To show his sincerity, he traveled to Washington D.C. at the end of July to meet with President Carter. Led by security advisor Abigniew Brzezinski, Carter's administration proposed a settlement based on the Brookings Institution Report of 1976. It was one of the very studies that Begin had dismissed out of hand. That Report proposed an agreement that focused on seemingly conflicting goals. They included the security of Israel, the freedom of the Arabs and the idea of an independent Palestinian government.

Begin hoped that he could prove the superiority of his plan to Carter. However, Carter did not approve of the plan that Begin offered. A reflection of Begin's beliefs, the plan did little more than express his basic ideals. It offered little in the way of concrete plans. Those who knew Begin understood his approach. To Carter's western mind, it was only a symbolic document, filled with over-blown legal language and little substance. The plan offered no detail regarding territorial disputes. It included no maps, no mention of Israel withdrawing from occupied territories, no proposals beyond vague statements that offered "peace for peace." Begin did write that Israel would not sanction withdrawals from the West Bank and the Gaza Strip.

An irritated Carter left his initial meeting with Begin understanding that the prime minister's commitment was to his own terms. His initial meeting with Begin confirmed his negative view. Begin, on the other hand, received Carter more positively. Rabin had warned Begin that Carter would be cold to the Israelis. He viewed Carter's attitude toward the Arabs as based on a mistaken belief that the Palestinian leaders were willing to make concessions. In reality, they were no more willing than the Israelis. Still, Begin could appreciate the President's idealism, being an idealist himself. Although Carter presented Begin's plan to Egyptian President Sadat, he knew Sadat would not accept it.

Carter immediately traveled to Geneva, Switzerland, to present his own peace settlement plan to the United Nations for support. He turned back to the ideas from the Brookings Institution. Carter hoped that various Arab delegations would meet around a table in Geneva. He wanted the U.S. and the United Soviet Socialist Republics to share the chairmanship of such a committee.

Sadat agreed with Begin on the unacceptability of such an idea. On November 9 standing before Egypt's parliament, Sadat proclaimed he would go "even to the Knesset in Jerusalem to discuss peace with Israel." That decision took courage, as it brought Sadat much criticism from his Arab neighbors. On November 11, Sadat received an invitation to visit Israel from Begin. Like Begin, Sadat enjoyed a good drama, and he agreed. Begin gave Sadat a welcome filled with grand ritual, despite the fact that the two countries remained technically at war.

A group of Israeli jets escorted Sadat's plane to Jerusalem's airport. At the airport, IDF units with polished weapons stood at stiff attention. Begin welcomed Sadat with warmth and idealistic words. He prepared a full reception for his visitor, leaving no detail unattended. While Sadat accepted the welcome graciously, he did not mince words with the Knesset. He chose his words not caring that he might offend some members of his audience. Sadat told the Israelis that he intended no more war, but that Israel must agree to return to the borders as they were in 1967; they would give up all occupied territories. He did not mention the PLO, but stressed the importance of Israel recognizing Palestinian rights. While he did not demand a Palestinian entity, or state, he clearly believed such a state should eventually develop. Begin supported Sadat's remarks with his own, when he told the Knesset, "We believe that if we achieve peace, true peace, we shall be able to assist one another in all realms of life, and a new era will be opened in the Middle East: an era of flourishing and growth, of development and progress and advancement, as in ancient times."

Anwar Sadat met with Begin in Jerusalem to discuss peace between Egypt and Israel. Sadat was candid when he spoke to the Knesset, making it clear that he wanted peace with Israel only if Israel returned to its pre-1967 borders.

Sadat did not even bring a written plan with him; however, he made his vision clear. He also made an unforgettable impression, on not only the Israelis, but also the world. Millions observed many of his activities by television. To the public, he appeared likable, joking with Golda Meir and his enemy, Ariel Sharon. The media loved him.

The meeting offered the two men a chance to take one another's measure. Begin knew they would reach no set agreement. The symbolism of the event made it worthwhile in his opinion. However, as President Carter continued to push for peace, Begin saw the security of Israel threatened, along with his dream of Eretz Israel. The very thing he had tried so hard to avoid, the threat of an independent Palestinian entity, seemed about to become a reality.

Rumors that Begin feared betrayal by Weizman and Dayan circulated. Additional speculation about his heart disease and diabetes fueled the rumor fires. For a time, he believed himself isolated, a lonely voice supporting Eretz Israel. Still, Dayan and Weizman accompanied him when he visited Ismailia, Egypt, in November. Sadat's reception did not incorporate the ritual and ceremony that Begin had offered him. Begin had hoped to visit Cairo, Egypt's capitol and Africa's largest city, but Sadat did not extend an invitation. Through such actions, Sadat reminded Begin that he not only led Egypt; he was also was a leader of the greater Arab world. In their meetings, Begin again spoke in general terms. He heaped complicated legal theory on Sadat, acting as a lawyer rather than a gracious statesman. The visit proved a failure.

To Begin's chagrin, the United States had closely observed the problems of Israel and Egypt. They simply could not agree on a peace plan. Begin felt Carter to be misguided, supportive of the PLO, and lacking in understanding of Jewish issues. He saw the U.S. president as being obsessed with "bringing peace to the Children of Abraham." In Carter's opinion, the Israelis proved unreasonable regarding territory, confusing physical borders with security. Conversely, Carter saw the Palestinians as an oppressed group that required rescue by an outside force. Yet, Begin and Carter also shared important aspects. Both had, as relative unknowns, won the highest offices in their respective countries. Both remained staunchly and unbendingly devoted to their religions. Ironically, that devotion to their ideals proved the very source of their political clashes. Whatever their opinions of one another, their fates had become entangled.

When President Carter met with Sadat in Aswan, Egypt in January of 1978, he appeared determined to go home with some type of set plan for peace. The agreement that developed, called the Aswan formula, incorporated many of the demands Sadat had already made. Those demands included the Palestinian entity, a phrase that Carter often repeated. Feeling insulted and belittled, Begin reacted to the pressure, continuing to refuse to "give in."

Begin did always behave courteously toward Sadat. No observable hostility existed between the two, but neither did any warmth or understanding. Begin admired Sadat as a formidable enemy, but he also regarded the man as first and foremost an Arab. Begin had no desire to understand his culture or ideals. He did agree to meet in the United States with Sadat and Carter, but he also ordered Weizman to meet with Sadat in July 1978. He hoped the meeting would lessen the influence of the United States, by building some trust for Israel on Sadat's part.

By the fall, Begin, Sadat, and Carter committed themselves to a meeting at Camp David by the year's end. Much correspondence passed back and forth. In September, Begin wrote to Carter that he agreed to place the question of removing the settlers from the northern and southern Sinai Peninsula before the Knesset. He then assured Carter that each member "will be enabled to vote in accordance with his own conscience."

With the world watching, an agreement was reached through the Camp David Accord. However, following the meeting, the peace seemed threatened by both Begin and Sadat, each of whom continued to struggle over a few points. Carter flew to the Middle East to talk with the men. Three months passed, and the negotiations remained unsigned. Then Begin agreed to visit Washington, but would not travel to Camp David. He wanted to avoid its symbolic significance as the origination of an American-guided plan for Middle

The peace established between Egypt and Israel through the Camp David Accord was tenuous at best, and President Carter had an important role in influencing Begin to resolve his differences with Sadat.

East peace. Carter became blunt, telling Begin that the peace quest would be a total failure if he did not sign.

Immovable, Begin arranged to fly back home. At the last moment, however, Sadat agreed to make a concession, and Begin returned to the White House. He accepted the compromise, but did not sign any formal agreement. Following a visit from Carter in March of 1978 designed to convince Begin to conclude the negotiation, Begin blasted the president in a political speech. In the end, it was Dayan who offered a legal solution to the stalemate. Begin seemed satisfied and agreed to sign. Whether he did so because he really believed in Dayan's solution, or just because the Israelis would receive the settlement credit is unknown.

Israel did not triumph over the Arabs in the agreement, and Begin could not celebrate a clear victory. However, the moment during which Begin met with Carter and Sadat in Washington in September of 1978 to sign three copies of the agreement proved satisfyingly dramatic. After working through twenty-three different drafts, Begin carried home a tentative plan for peace.

The Camp David Accord outlined two frameworks for peace, one between Israel and Egypt, and another, not to be acted upon until 1981. It included Israel's additional Arab neighbors. Although Israel agreed to withdraw full military government from the Gaza Strip and the West Bank, it could keep a military contingent there for purposes of security. Residents of those territories could set up their own governments over the next five years. In return for withdrawing from the Sinai Peninsula, Israel gained the right to exist peacefully with its Arab neighbors.

Begin must have felt a long way from the words of prayer he had uttered during his first visit to the Wailing Wall in 1967: "Our enemies encompassed us about, yea they encompassed us about and arose to destroy us as a people. Yet has their counsel been destroyed and their schemes will not be accomplished."

However, that December, when he jointly shared the 1978 Nobel Peace Prize with Anwar Sadat, Begin could not contain his pride. He had achieved a title, that of Nobel Laureate, that no other Israeli statesman could claim.

Aase Lionaes, Chairman of the Norwegian Nobel Committee, delivered the Nobel awards speech on December 10, 1978. He noted the "audacious hope" represented by the award, a hope of peace, not only for Israel and Egypt, but also for the entire Middle East. In part, Lionaes told his audience, "we only know of one previous peace agreement between Egypt and Israel. This, as Israeli scholars have revealed, took place some 3,000 years ago; it was the peace concluded between King David's son, wise King Solomon, and the Egyptian Pharaoh." The comparisons of those great men to Begin and Sadat obviously flattered both men. Then he added, "It is for their work in laying a foundation for future peace between these two one-time enemy countries that the President of Egypt, Anwar al-Sadat, and the Prime Minister of Israel, Menachem Begin, have been honoured with the Nobel Peace Prize for 1978."

While Sadat did not attend the awards ceremony in Oslo, Norway, Begin did. He would need the joy that such a distinguished accomplishment brought. It would help him to stand the many challenges to his office in the years that would follow.

Begin (right), Sadat (left), and Carter shake hands after signing the Camp David Accord. However, Israeli politicians did not immediately agree with the terms of the agreement.

6

A Time
of Dissent

Menachem Begin was the first Israeli statesman to make peace with Egypt. He had also managed, in his opinion, to preserve Judea and Samaria for Eretz Israel. But when he returned home, he faced anger and dissent in the Knesset. Now new voices joined the opposition, voices belonging to one-time Begin supporters. Apparently, everyone except Sharon hated the Egypt-Israel agreement. Eventually, however, the Knesset approved the outline.

In February of 1979, Begin and Sadat returned yet again to Washington to work on a final draft that ended in disagreement. In March, Begin traveled back to the states for a serious talk with President Carter, who later visited Sadat in Cairo and then Begin in Jerusalem. Following Carter's persuasion, both men signed a final draft and returned with Carter to Washington. There, they sealed their agreement. In another crucial ceremony, the men signed the Camp David Accord at the White House on March 26, 1979. A joint letter from Begin and Sadat, addressed to President Carter, read in part:

> The two Governments agree to negotiate continuously and in good faith to conclude these negotiations at the earliest possible date. They also agree that the objective of the negotiations is the establishment of the self-governing authority in the West Bank and Gaza in order to provide full autonomy to the inhabitants. Israel and Egypt set for themselves the goal of completing the negotiations within one year so that elections will be held as expeditiously as possible after agreement has been reached between the parties . . . The Israel military government and its civilian administration will be withdrawn, to be replaced by the self-governing authority, as specified in the "Framework for Peace in the Middle East."

The letter was signed "Yours sincerely," followed by Begin's and Sadat's names.

After all of the excitement, Begin appeared depressed. He looked worried and exhausted, and none of his former spirit remained. Again rumors circulated regarding his poor health. At year's end, his own contingent, or supporters, attacked him. Weizman joined Sharon and a third man, David Levy, in an attempt to unseat Begin. For a time, Begin's depression threatened to leave him silent and accepting of the move to oust him. But when the trio suggested that Begin should retire, he suddenly came to life to prevent their "coup," or taking over, of his position. Within months, however, he had again slipped into depression. Speculation regarding the damage caused by his diabetes and heart disease filled the local papers.

In addition to threats from within his party, Begin had to deal with an ongoing threat by the PLO. It was stationed in the country of Lebanon. Lebanon, a country north of Israel

Yasir Arafat and the Palestinian Liberation Organization (PLO) began their opposition to Begin and the Israelis in 1978 with the murder of 37 Israelis on the road between Tel Aviv and Haifa. Begin responded with Operation Litani.

on the eastern coast of the Mediterranean Sea, had also suffered internal fighting, a Civil War, between Christian and Muslims since 1975. Its instability allowed other countries to use it as a base for attacking Israel. Following its 1970 expulsion from Jordan, the PLO established its main base in the southern part of Lebanon. In March of 1978, a group from Lebanon killed 37 people on the road between two of Israel's important cities, Tel Aviv and the seaport of Haifa. Begin answered the challenge and retaliated in an act called

Operation Litani, named for the Litani River. He had to withdraw his forces, though, when pressured by the United States to do so. U.N. forces entered Lebanon instead, embarrassing the Begin government.

As a result, Moshe Dayan resigned his foreign minister post in 1979. Ezer Weizman followed him in 1980. Begin wrote to Weizman, acknowledging his resignation on May 26. He scolded his former defense minister, accusing him, "out of impatience and rashness," of trying to remove Begin from office, openly on television, "as well as by intrigue." He told Weizman flatly that he had failed to take advantage of a rare opportunity to serve his country due to an "ambition that is mind-numbing."

As a bright spot for Begin, in 1980 aspects of the peace negotiations with Egypt were completed. Egypt and Israel exchanged ambassadors and opened embassies. Begin reminded his people that Egypt, Israel's largest potential Arab enemy, with the biggest military force, remained at peace with their country.

Begin also had to deal with the Arab country of Iraq and its president, Saddam Hussein, to whom Begin referred as "the Butcher of Baghdad." Under Hussein, a PLO advocate, a nuclear reactor went into construction in Osirak, Iraq. Begin regarded the project as a deadly weapon that threatened Israel's well-being. Destruction of the reactor would send a clear message to Hussein that Israel would fight his ambition to dominate the Persian Gulf. Begin had no intention of allowing Hussein to inflict an instant holocaust, using a nuclear weapon against Israel. He stated to his cabinet and to the world, "there will be no other Holocaust in this century."

Actions against Lebanese forces escalated in 1981. Syrian president Assad ordered his forces to protect Syria's safety by bombing Zahlan, a city close to the road that connected Beirut and Damascus. Because Begin considered Zahlan a friendly city, an ally, Israeli aircraft destroyed two Syrian helicopters.

Assad responded by moving more arms in the forms of missiles into Zahlan. Once again, Begin bowed to the pressure of the United States when President Ronald Reagan insisted that Israel not destroy the Syrian missiles. And once again, Begin, as Israel's political head, embarrassed his country by agreeing. Many Israelis wondered where the Begin of 1977, who had sworn to have a tough security policy, had gone.

The June 1981 Knesset elections featured attacks on the Likud for failing to halt the PLO buildup in Lebanon. Begin's position as prime minister remained shaky, and his reelection seemed unlikely. However, three weeks prior to the election, the IDF attacked and destroyed the Osirak nuclear reactor. Although many countries expressed anger and dismay, Israel's citizens seemed to approve. Simultaneously, the Likud reduced taxes on luxury goods, triggering a public spending spree that helped convince voters to support the party. Most importantly, once again Begin came to life—the "Old Man" rallied his supporters with his legendary rhetoric.

One story told by a Begin acquaintance gives an example of the prime minister's skill at working crowds. Forty-eight hours before the election, the Labor party organized a huge rally at the Tel Aviv city hall. The leading members of the party sat on a platform, listening to a comedian warm up the crowd. He welcomed them to the rally. Then he said it was a pleasure to see "Real Israelis," rather than the "cooks and gatekeepers and *chach-chachs*" who hung out at Likud's headquarters.

Begin, who did not keep up with Israeli slang, had to ask a friend the meaning of the phrase. *Chach-Chach*, he was told, represented an insult against north African Jews. It meant "red neck" or "trash." On the night before the election, Begin dramatically addressed his supporters, informing them of the name-calling. "Is that what you are?" he demanded of the frenzied crowd. "No!" they screamed back. Now the election was not only political, it had become personal. Begin once again manipulated his audience, and they loved him for it.

While Israel's attack on Iraq's nuclear reactor brought a worldwide outcry, it did not hurt Begin's party at home. The Likud won the election. The Labor party, however, gained 15 seats for a total of 47, representing a sizeable increase in its political power. Still, at sixty-seven years of age Begin had again proved victorious. He had to make an important choice following the divisive election. He could choose to work to unite the country, or he could continue to move toward his goal of Eretz Israel by removing the Palestinian threat permanently. He chose the latter course. Unfortunately, it would not make him a father of Israel, but rather a father of tragedy that touched tens of thousands of people.

Sharon became Begin's new minister of defense, supported by his chief of staff, General Eitan. Both were aggressive military figures, and they decided the military policy for Israel. In July of 1981, the PLO bombed Israel, which responded by bombing PLO strongholds in southern Lebanon. Begin had in mind not only victory, but also the signing of a peace treaty with a second Arab nation, Lebanon. He did not, however, take into account the fact that he challenged not a unified nation run from a central government in Beirut, but many different factions. The various rivals for power included groups such as the Suni, Shia, Maronite and Greek Orthodox Christians. In addition, various political radicals and conservatives controlled business interests in an approach similar to that of Sicily's mafia.

The United States interceded in its usual pattern, establishing a temporary peace. Later, Sharon would decide to focus on Beirut, Lebanon's capital, even though in the past, the Israelis had believed that occupying an Arab capital could lead to disaster. Sharon and Begin saw the possibility of forming an alliance with friendly forces inside Lebanon. Various Lebanon Christian groups volunteered to help Israel defeat and oust the PLO from their country. Such strategy made clear Begin's lack of knowledge regarding the political and military Arab culture.

While he did not want to go to war with Syria, that country provided Lebanon's dominant Arab force. Now war between Syria, the PLO and Israel seemed a certainty.

As Begin struggled with threats from outside his country, he appeared again depressed. Even in publicized events, he made little effort to hide or compensate for his obvious decline. He spent more time at home with Aliza, herself in poor health. She had always served as his best, and sometimes his only, friend and confidant. Begin became little more than a figurehead for his government, which others stepped in to run.

On October 6, 1981, Begin received crushing news. His one-time enemy, then fellow negotiator, Anwar Sadat had been assassinated. He had been shot down by members of his own military. Begin attended the Cairo funeral, walking to the Saturday event. In respect for the Jewish Sabbath, he could not ride in the limousines provided for diplomats.

By June of 1982, Sharon had invaded Lebanon in a move called Operation Peace for Galilee. Sharon hoped to weaken the PLO and support Israel's Christian allies in Lebanon. He wanted to occupy Beirut, Lebanon's capitol city. But Operation Peace for Galilee represented the first war not supported by Israel's public. While the public had viewed the wars of 1948, 1967, and 1973 as necessary for Israel's survival, it did not see the latest offensive in that way. For the first time, Israel did not act in self-defense. Instead, it went on the offensive, attacking awithout being first attacked. The change in attitude proved crucial. As Israeli casualties grew, Begin's administration drew sharp criticism. While Israel succeeded in weakening the PLO, it achieved no clear victory and suffered the loss of many in the IDF. The public saw Sharon as having manipulated Begin, "The Old Man," into war.

Begin had underestimated Sharon's effect on the voting public. While a celebrated war hero, Sharon represented a poor politician, one who should not be establishing public policy.

Defense Minister Ariel Sharon points to a map to explain Israel's objective during Operation Peace for Galilee. The invasion of Lebanon was an act of aggression by Israel, and was not supported by the Israeli public.

Although Begin did not recognize that fact, Israel's people did, and many expressed little faith in Sharon's ability to make logical decisions about war. He did not have Dayan's cool head, and he remained too emotional to properly handle the power Begin had given him. Along with the other "hawks," or war supporters in Begin's second cabinet, Foreign Minister Yitzhak Shamir and Treasury Minister Yoram Aridor, Sharon actively sought war. The cabinet succeeded in basically usurping Begin's power, and critics later called the years 1981-1983 "Begin's Demise."

Begin watched as Sharon continued his push to take over Beirut. Israel's public image became more negative as the world learned of the enormous casualties involved in the siege of

Beirut. The PLO continued to hang on to the city where its leader, Yasir Arafat, would not yield. The United States sent its special ambassador, Philip Habib, in an attempt to convince Begin of the need for peace. Habib also emphasized the strain that the Israeli attacks placed on Israel's relationship with the United States.

Understanding that he stood isolated from Arab support, Arafat agreed to a deal, set up by the American, Habib. The agreement allowed about 10,000 PLO forces to leave Beirut under the protection of the United States. In order to protect remaining Palestinian refugees, a group of U.S. Marines would stay behind. Begin liked the plan. He saw it as substituting Marines for IDF to offer Israel a protective buffer from Lebanon. However, Sharon disagreed. He called for total destruction of southern Beirut, claiming it should be "razed to the ground." Ronald Reagan warned Begin of "serious consequences," should the attacks continue. Begin retorted, "Jews do not kneel except to God." But by August of 1982, Begin himself doubted Sharon's ability to continue military command. He certainly had proved a terrible politician, having insulted Habib and his fellow diplomats on multiple occasions.

By September, the estimates of the dead and wounded included hundreds of Syrians dead with more than 1,000 wounded; 1,000 Palestinians dead, with 7,000 captured; 17,825 Lebanese dead and more than 30,000 wounded, and 344 Israelis dead with more than 2,000 wounded. More would have to die to awaken Begin to the horror of the war.

With Arafat and the PLO out of Beirut, Christians controlled Lebanon. They elected a new president, Bashir Gemayel on August 23, 1982. Begin had difficulty dealing with Gemayel, charging him with lack of support during the Israeli siege of Beirut. Gemayel tried to reach an agreement with Begin. While he stated that his identity as an Arab meant he stood politically with Arab states, he made clear that he personally supported Begin. He would even work with Begin, acting as a representative to his fellow Arabs. On September 1, when Ronald Reagan announced a plan for Middle East peace, Begin's frustration mounted. He did not desire further negotiations with the PLO, a group he felt his country had defeated.

Begin could have pulled all IDF troops from Lebanon, but he did not. Then, on September 12, his administration received a crippling blow by an incident known as the Sabra-Shatilla massacre. Between three and four hundred Christian militiamen surrounded two Palestinian refugee camps named Sabra and Shatilla. Over about forty-eight hours, 700-800 Palestinians died—men, women and children. Although the IDF claimed they did not play a direct roll in the attack, having ordered their own soldiers not to enter the camp, IDF officers watched the entire operation from a sixth-story rooftop. Sharon immediately learned of the terrible event, but no one bothered to inform Begin until the following day. On top of that extraordinary event came another. On September 14, assassins killed the newly elected Lebanon president Gemayel and his entire staff by blowing up their apartment house.

Sharon clearly had knowledge of the Christians' desire to enter the camps, which they believed might harbor PLO members. No longer able to avoid his duties, Begin removed Sharon from his minister post, although he allowed him to remain in the cabinet. Begin himself had once stated, "Sharon is a great general . . . and a vicious character."

The new defense minister, Moshe Arens, wanted Israel's immediate withdrawal from Lebanon. The IDF did pull back, but found itself caught in a cross fire of warring internal groups. A new group, the Shias from southern Lebanon, had been antagonized by the long Israeli occupation of their country. In November of 1983, Shias destroyed the Israeli post in Tyre. Between January and June of 1985, the IDF pulled out of Lebanon, leaving only a token group to patrol a narrow zone for security.

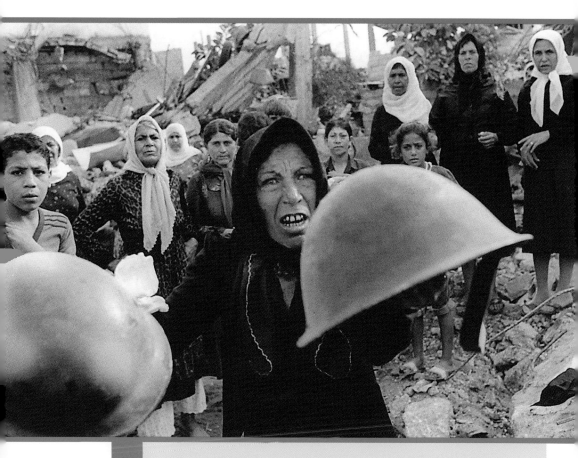

This Palestinian woman survived the Sabra-Shatilla massacre in Lebanon. Although Israeli troops did not take part in the massacre that resulted in the deaths of over 700 people, they did watch as Christian militiamen entered the refugee camp and slaughtered the Palestinians.

The war proved a crushing blow to Begin, already physically and emotionally weakened by disease, age and disappointment. Later scholars chose the Lebanon War as an example of a fundamental fact: Israel was not just a victim of its enemies, as Begin often claimed. It was also a victim of its own dreams and ideals. The dreams of security and expansion led to an illusion, one advanced by Israel's own leaders. Those leaders believed war represented the best chance for Israel's advancement, but sometimes those wars did not reap the benefits the people thought they might. Israel's attack against Lebanon was not an attack against an organized government. Rather, it represented an attack against terrorists, a group very difficult to destroy. Also, in the Lebanon War, Israel provoked Syria, a country that became its bitterest enemy. The war actually increased Syria's influence in Lebanon.

Without knowing it, Begin's IDF taught Syria a valuable lesson about its military weaknesses and how to overcome them. In hopes of preserving the occupation of the West Bank, Begin placed too much power in the hands of his military leaders. Even had Begin succeeded in ousting the Syrians from Lebanon, his troops could not possibly have then occupied the entire country to prevent their enemy's return.

Begin could not defend himself by claiming ignorance or by blaming his military. He could hardly blame Sharon alone. He may have chosen not to involve himself, but he still bore ultimate responsibility as head of state.

Later, a group called the Israeli Kahan Commission formally examined Sharon's actions. Its members found Sharon to blame for poor judgment, as he did not foresee disaster when he approved the Christians' entrance into the Palestinian camps. The Commission also detected no agreement between Israel's political and military leaders to commit the atrocities. Such slaughters were not unprecedented. Lebanese Christians and Palestinian Muslims had on several occasions massacred each other's populations. Syrian President Hafez Assad slaughtered more than 20,000 Muslim civilians in one attack. Keeping these facts in mind, the commission basically ruled that Sharon should have anticipated and stopped the disaster, but that he could not be charged of any official crime.

Due to Sharon's actions and Begin's lack of military leadership, Begin lost the loyalty of his troops and the approval of much of Israel's public. His own officers no longer treated him respectfully, yet Begin showed little response to the shift in his reputation. While he may have been appalled by Sharon's actions, he outwardly seemed not to care much about the massacre that shocked the world. He even stated, "We've known worse crises."

Begin's reaction was simple retreat into his own world. One reporter in a February 1982, *Washington Post* article stated that the prime minister suffered "from a depression from which he can't recover." Begin's advisors, Uri Porath and Yehiel Kadishai labeled the story "gossip" and "a vicious act of malice." They admitted that Begin seemed unable to sit still for long periods, but they also claimed that he remained in total control of important matters of state. As time passed, everyone doubted their claims.

Begin suffered difficulties in his personal life as well as his political career. His wife, Aliza, died of lung cancer in 1982.

7

An Aged Warrior

Menachem Begin ended 1982 with an even more crushing blow than the one dealt his political life by the Sabra-Shatilla massacre. While in Los Angeles, California, in November, he learned of the death of his beloved wife from lung cancer. For forty-three years, Aliza had been the only person he trusted, and his devotion to her had never wavered. He cried when he received the news from his daughter Leah, then recited from Proverbs: "I shall remember you going after me on an unseen desert."

Following Aliza's death, Begin became as much of a recluse as possible. He appeared in public mainly to attend funerals and other ceremonies. As Israel remained divided over the aftermath of the Lebanon War, Begin came as close as he ever would to admitting that he had, perhaps, made a mistake in supporting Sharon and his military actions. In 1983, he urged his countrymen to "show tolerance," to "rid themselves of hatred and show understanding" in their dealings with one another. He added, "differences of opinion were legitimate and should not lead to physical confrontation."

During his final one hundred days in office, Begin supported all of the rumors of his frailty with his reclusive ways. Friends did not see him for weeks, and then were shocked by his gaunt appearance when they did meet with him. While Porath and Kadishai did their best to shield their own powers from public knowledge, most people understood that Begin no longer actually ran the country. He avoided at all costs face-to-face meetings and would not see friends or be a part of crucial dealings. Menachem Begin clearly had reached the end of his political career.

As Begin ignored the country's problems, inflation, causing Israel's money to lose its buying power, gripped Israel. The volume of products that it produced decreased, while prices skyrocketed. From 1948 through 1972, Israel's inflation could be measured in single digits; it never grew even to 10%. By 1984, it would increase to a high of 445%. Begin had to take credit for the last few of those years of increase. Oil prices also skyrocketed between 1973 and 1982. Egypt returned to drill in the Sinai oil fields in 1979, a year in which prices rose so much. The Arabs threatened to devastate the Israeli economy. They made good on their word. Losses to the economy between 1973 and 1982 were an estimated 12 billion dollars worth. Every Israeli citizen suffered due to the lack of a strong economic policy.

Public opinion of Begin proved unkind. The ever-present rumors now labeled him not merely ill and depressed, but "deranged." People even studied his signature and pronounced it the writing of a tortured man. In June of 1983, he announced that he would soon resign. He chose his successor, Foreign Minister Yitzhak Shamir, but continued to control the government, not officially submitting a resignation to the Knesset. Although many agreed that Begin should leave, they also agreed that no one in the Knesset, neither in Begin's cabinet nor in the opposition, possessed the Old Man's rapport with the public. His mysterious but undisputed charisma continued.

Begin's routine changed little. Each day he worked for several hours in the morning. His afternoons included long naps before retiring. He did attend cabinet meetings on Sunday, but continued to avoid his friends and all serious concerns. Between September and November, Begin appeared in not one photograph.

Three months passed after Begin's announced retirement. On September 14, 1983, Begin went about his daily routine as on any other day. He had decided that would be his final day in office, but he warned no one. Left with no true confidants, now that Aliza and his past political supporters were gone, Begin had no one to tell.

Before departing home for his cabinet meeting, Begin drank a cup of tea. In the past, Aliza had brought him his tea; now Leah, who lived with him, fulfilled that duty. As usual, he listened to the BBC, British programs, on the radio and read several morning papers, written in Hebrew, followed by other papers from Europe. He met his driver at 8:00 A.M. and climbed into the ten-year old Ford he had inherited from Rabin.

A long-time Begin acquaintance recorded the activities of the prime minister's final day. After a preliminary meeting with Defense Minister Moshe Arens and other officials, Begin walked to the head of the cabinet table. Porath helped him make his way slowly to the position of power. Begin read a list of important items, but commented little. By 10:30 A.M., the meetings had ended. He returned to his office for an additional two hours of reading, ignoring knocks on his office door. By 1:30, he wanted to return home for his favorite meal of boiled chicken and vegetables. He arose from his nap at 4:00 and received a bundle of reports from Kadishai requiring his approval.

On September 15, reporters wanted to know Begin's future plans. They thought he might visit President Chaim Herzog and help promote the political future of both the old and new members of the Herut. He had little interest in either activity. He did remind his aides to remove the portraits of Herzl and Jabotinsky from his office, along with other items and a family photograph. He wondered aloud whether there might be a place on the office wall, amid the portraits of former prime ministers, for his own. After another look around, he left to visit his son.

Begin spent the following months entirely secluded. He could be seen in public only at memorials held for Aliza or at weddings for some of his eight grandchildren. Leah remained devoted to her father, staying at his side. Kadishai visited the apartment every day to help Begin continue his correspondence. He received a few friends and followed his son Benjamin's political career, as a leader in the Likud party.

Despite Begin's disappearance from public view, his influence was evident in the 1984 elections, both in a positive and negative way. Some Sephardic Jews continued to support the Likud, specifically because it was Begin's party. Most of those voters came from immigrant families, families like Begin's own who were not native to Israel. One emotional voter declared, "Because of Begin, we can hold our heads up. Begin did that for me. The Likud, even without Begin, is still Begin. I'll never forget what he meant to me and my family." However, not everyone felt this positive. During a conference in New York City, one young woman stated bluntly that Begin and the Likud had ruined her country and that she and her family felt like strangers in their own land. In the 1984 election, the Sephardis again supported the Likud, even without Begin. But the passion present in past elections was missing, along with the party's past leader.

The 1984 election represented a new situation. No party won a clear majority of seats in the Knesset, so the Likud and the Labor Party in a national unity government had to share governing duties. Shamir represented the Likud, while Shimon

Begin became a recluse after his wife's death, and rarely appeared in public. He is seen here with his son and daughter at Aliza's funeral in 1982.

Peres represented Labor. Peres would hold the office of prime minister for 25 months while Shamir served as foreign minister, then the two would exchange positions for an additional 25 months. Even by 1988, no clear winner emerged in an election, and another national unity government began. This time, Shamir served as prime minister for the entire four years. However, for the first time in history, the prime minister received a vote of no confidence from the Knesset in 1990, meaning the members no longer wanted Shamir as leader. He was forced out of office, but because no strong charismatic leader appeared as a replacement, he returned to power later that year. Clearly, Begin's exit from politics began a new chapter in Israel's story.

On March 3, 1992, Begin collapsed and was rushed to the

Begin's health continued to deteriorate, and in 1992 he suffered a heart attack from which he never recovered. Kadishai and Begin's family were by his side when he died, as hundreds of well-wishers waited outside the hospital for news of their former prime minister.

hospital. At first, doctors believed he had suffered a stroke. After 20 hours in a coma, he regained consciousness. Testing indicated he had suffered a heart attack, and a pacemaker placed inside his heart on March 5 helped control his heartbeat. Hundreds of well-wishers stood outside during Begin's last few days, but only his family and Kadishai were allowed visits. They were at his side when he died at age 79.

The hospital rabbi recited a brief prayer, and the death was officially announced. Begin had left instructions that no large state funeral be held. He chose instead a simple Jewish burial ceremony with no eulogies, speeches of public praise, planned. Shamir did deliver two speeches, one to the nation by radio, and another to the cabinet. Shamir termed Begin "one of the great men," reminding his listeners of Begin's idealism. He promised that, "In the spirit of his doctrine and path, we will continue the struggle for the sake of the strengthening of the Jewish people in its land."

Begin's burial ceremony at graveside on the Mount of Olives remained simple, but the funeral itself attracted an estimated 75,000 mourners. Many cried as they walked two and a half miles along the road from the funeral home to the cemetery. Others rode in a group of 50 busses, the only traffic allowed on the streets. Benjamin Begin took care that his father's wishes were carried out; Begin desired a traditional Jewish funeral, not an international spectacle. President Chaim Herzog, Prime Minister Shamir, Labor Party Chairman Rabin and many other politicians, including the Egyptian Ambassador, stood at the grave with Benjamin, Leah and Hasia. U.S. President George H. W. Bush stated about Begin that, "his historic role in the peace process will never be forgotten."

Begin is probably remembered most for his peace negotiations with Egypt; although he earned some measure of success in ensuring peace for Israel, critics claim that he neglected his country's domestic affairs in doing so.

8

Menachem Begin's Legacy

Historians continue to debate Begin's importance to Israel and to the world. He made major changes in Israel and the Middle East but did not achieve all of his set goals. He did return the Sinai to Egypt, but hoped, in turn, to reclaim Judea and Samaria. Very early during his service to his country, he had stated, "I want to be remembered as the man who set the borders of Eretz Yisraeil for all eternity." He did not succeed. Begin did, however, strengthen the West Bank and the Golan Heights, which proved imperative to the safety of Israel.

Always mindful of the symbolic, Begin removed the British pound, a symbol of Israel's pre-state occupation, as Israel's official unit of currency. He replaced it with the shekel, a coin used by the ancient Hebrews. Such links to tradition remained of huge importance for Begin's vision of Israel. Although he was not a native-born Israeli, he constantly reminded those who were of their historic roots. In a move with a similar motive, Begin led the Knesset to declare all of Jerusalem, previously divided (prior to the 1967 War) into Israeli and Jewish sectors, the nation's eternal capital. He maintained a lifelong attitude toward Jerusalem as Israel's holy city and its civic seat, although most other governments would not recognize it as such, due to Arab claims on the area. In a memorial for Begin, one speaker explained Begin's effect by saying that he:

> . . . closed the gap in Israel's public life between Israeli civil society and Jewish tradition. Every society has a civil religion, those symbols and expressions which are the property of the commonality of the whole country and which evoke the emotions that make people feel that they belong to each other and to the country. . . . Labor tried to separate . . . traditional Judaism from the expressions and the symbols of the new Israel. Begin ended that.

Despite his love for the ideal of a unified religious Israel, Begin never actually "walked the land" to get to know his people. He remained an outsider, and younger Israelis saw him as they did their parents and grandparents, part of a lost generation, one they made fun of. The conservative Sephardim, made up of members of the great migration to Israel from the 1950s, became his greatest supporters.

Perhaps Begin's greatest weakness was his refusal to even try to understand the Arabs. Unlike his predecessor, David Ben-Gurion, and his political opponent and later cabinet member, Moshe Dayan, Begin lacked any great curiosity about Arabs. While Ben-Gurion and Dayan both became students of Arab culture, Begin had no desire to learn their language or read their literature. To him, members of the PLO were only a new version of the Nazis.

Certainly he is best remembered for his peace dealings with Egypt. One of Israel's finest educational institutions, Bar-Ilan University in Tel Aviv, has a Begin-Sadat Center for Strategic

Studies where the effects of the two men are formally studied. In the decades since the Camp David Accord, trade and other interchange between Israel and Egypt has not increased. In the opinion of some, Egypt never really desired a relationship with Israel—it settled on peace out of fear of its neighbor. The peace agreement proved of great strategic benefit to both countries, but it in no way normalized relationships between them.

The peace treaty allowed Begin to satisfy his lifelong desire for recognition, particularly with his winning of the Nobel Peace Prize. Even so, his reputation suffered from the later Lebanon War. And while he is remembered as the founder of the Herut Party, when Begin died, the party's ideals also died. His strong personality kept the Herut in power. No leader of any party emerged in the decades following Begin's death who could match his charisma and talent for energizing an audience.

In the end, Begin's legacy remains a mixed one. His peace efforts with the Arabs and his determination to realize Eretz Israel also caused him to neglect the internal problems of his own country. He did not supply the economic and labor leadership sorely needed by the Israelis. He also let himself be misled by his own cabinet members, particularly Sharon, causing himself embarrassment on several occasions. The most telling act made by Begin may have been his resignation. He knew when to quit, an acknowledgement that escapes many great men.

Perhaps the best words to recall Menachem Begin are those that accompanied the awards for the Nobel Peace Prize on December 10, 1978. The chairman of the Norwegian Nobel Committee, Aase Lionaes, spoke of both Sadat and Begin in his lengthy speech. He concluded by saying, "May I express the hope that this Nobel Peace Prize ceremony, enacted in our small and wintry country, tucked away near the Arctic Circle, may provide an enduring reminder to the world that it was here that representatives of Egypt and Israel shook hands as they celebrated the greatest of all victories—conciliation and lasting peace based on respect for human rights and human dignity."

1913 Born Menachem Wolfovitch Begin on August 16, 1913 in Brest-Litovsk, Poland

1929 Joins Betar youth movement

1935 Granted law degree from Warsaw University

1938 Appointed head of Betar, Poland

1939 Marries Aliza (Ola) Arnold on May 29

Flees Warsaw for Vilna

1940 Arrested by N.K.V.D.

1941 Sentenced to eight years in Siberian prison camp—sentence later commuted—discovers parents and two siblings died in Nazi prison camps

1942 Travels to Palestine as interpreter in Polish Army and joins Eliza

1943 Becomes leader of Etzel/Irgun, a Jewish underground movement

Son Benjamin Ze'ev born

1944-1948 Leads terrorist attacks against British and Arabs

1946 Daughter Hasia born

1948 State of Israel formalized—Begin founds Herut political party

1949 Elected to Knesset as conservative

Daughter Leah born

1965 Merges Herut with a liberal party to form future Likud Party

1967 Six-Day War—becomes member of New National Unity Government

1970 Resigns over disagreement about American Peace Plan initiative

1973 Elected head of Likud party—plagued by health problems

1977 Elected prime minister of Israel—begins peace talks with Egypt

1978 Signs Camp David Peace Accord with Egypt's Anwar Sadat

Shares Nobel Peace Prize with Anwar Sadat

1979 Peace Treaty with Egypt signed—battles with PLO begin

1980 Israel Air Force destroys nuclear reactor in Osirak near Baghdad

Party struggles for re-election

1981	Rumors of failing health denied
1982	War of Lebanon—Aliza dies in November
1983	Resigns as Prime Minister on September 15
1984–1992	Lives as recluse, seeing mainly children and grandchildren
1992	Dies on March 9

Abadi, Jacob. *Israel's Leadership: from Utopia to Crisis.* Westport, CT: Greenwood Press, 1993.

Begin, Menachem. *White Nights: The Story of a Prisoner in Russia.* 1957. Trans. Katie Kaplan. New York: Harper & Row, 1977.

Chafets, Ze'ev. *Heroes and Hustlers, Hard Hats and Holy Men: Inside the New Israel.* New York: William Morrow and Co., Inc., 1986.

Elazar, Daniel J. "In Memoriam—Menachem Begin." *Jerusalem Center for Public Affairs.* n.d. 01 Nov 01 *http://www.jepa.org/dje/articles/mbegin.htm.*

Feron, James. "Menachem Begin, Guerrilla Leader Who Became Peacemaker." *The New York Times on the Web* 03 Oct. 92. 01 Nov. 01 *http://www.nytimes.com/learning/general/onthisday/bday/0816.html.*

Harkabi, Yehoshafat. *Israel's Fateful Hour.* Trans. Lenn Schramm. New York: Harper & Row, 1988.

"Menachem Begin: Prime Minister of Israel 1877-1983." State of Israel Homepage. 1999. 01 Nov. 01 *http://www.israel.org.*

Metz, Helen Chapin, ed. *Israel: a country study.* Washington D.C.: Library of Congress, 1990.

Perlmutter, Amos. *The Life and Times of Menachem Begin.* New York: Doubleday, 1987.

Abdullah, King of Jordan, 41
Abraham, 16-17
Allah, 17
Altalena, 42
Arab-Israeli conflict
    and Arabs in Palestine, 18, 32-33
    and Begin, 28, 31-35, 40, 44, 46, 51-
        52, 58, 76-79, 80-87, 89, 98, 99
    Begin *vs.* Ben-Gurion on, 34
    and Egypt, 42-43, 44, 46, 48, 49, 52-54
    and Iraq, 53, 78, 80
    and Israeli statehood, 32
    and Jordan, 41, 42, 46, 48, 49, 53
    and Lebanon, 76-79, 80-87
    in Palestine, 20-22, 31-35
    and PLO, 54, 56, 76-78, 79, 80-87
    religious origins of, 14, 16-17
    and Six-Day War, 15, 46, 48, 49
    and Syria, 46, 48, 49, 52-54, 78-79,
        81-87
    and Yom Kippur War, 52-54
Arabs
    Begin *versus,* 28, 31-35, 40
    in Israel, 39-40
    in Palestine, 18, 32-33
Arafat, Yasir, 83
Arens, Moshe, 84, 91
Assad, Hafez, 65, 78-79, 86
Aswan formula, 70

Bader, Yohanan, 38, 39
Begin, Aliza (Ola) Arnold (wife), 22,
    25, 26, 27, 28, 31, 45, 89, 91, 92
Begin, Benjamin Ze'ev (son), 31, 40,
    92, 95
Begin, Dov Zeev (father), 18, 20, 31
Begin, Hasia (daughter), 31, 40, 95
Begin, Leah (daughter), 31, 40, 89, 91,
    92, 95
Begin, Menachem
    and anti-British/Arab activities, 28,
        31-35, 40, 61
    and Arab-Israeli conflict, 28, 31-35,
        40, 44, 46, 51-52, 58, 76-79, 80-87,
        89, 98, 99

and arrest by N.K.V.D., 23, 26-28
Ben-Gurion *vs.,* 31, 34, 37, 38-39,
    40-41, 42, 43, 48
and Betar Youth movement, 20
birth of, 18
and cabinet, 59-61, 63-65, 78, 81-82,
    83, 84, 91, 99
childhood of, 20
children of, 31, 40, 89, 91, 92, 95
and choice of president, 58-59
and daily life, 40, 45-46, 91
death of, 95, 99
and death of family in Nazi camps,
    30, 31, 40
and depression, 56, 87
and economy, 90, 99
education of, 20, 22
and Egypt, 44
family of, 18, 20, 30, 31
and flight from Warsaw to Vilna,
    22
and Gahal, 45, 46, 49, 52
and grandchildren, 92
as head of Betar, Poland, 22
and health problems, 14, 15, 55, 59,
    69, 76, 85, 93, 95
and Herut party, 34, 37, 38, 41, 42,
    43-45, 46, 49, 57, 59, 99
and inaction as weakness, 22
and Israeli currency, 97
and Jerusalem, 98
in Jewish underground movement,
    31-33, 34, 40, 42
in Knesset, 38, 46
legacy of, 97-99
and Likud party, 52, 54, 56, 57-58,
    59, 79, 80, 92
marriage of, 22, 25, 26, 27, 28, 31,
    40, 45, 89, 91
and national unity government,
    46-49, 51
and 1984 elections, 92-93
and Nobel Peace Prize, 73, 99
and occupied territories, 51-52, 54,
    58, 61, 64, 65, 66, 72, 75, 86, 97

in Palestine as interpreter in Polish
   Army, 18, 30
and peace process with Egypt, 13-16,
   52, 61, 63, 64-65, 66-70, 72-73,
   75-76, 78, 98-99
in Poland, 18-22, 25
as prime minister, 15, 22, 51-52,
   54-61
as recluse, 89-90, 92
and retirement, 90-92, 99
and united land of Israel, 15, 22,
   27, 30, 31-35, 41, 46, 51, 54,
   60-61, 69, 80, 97, 98, 99, 655
and Zionism, 20-22, 27
Ben-Gurion, David, 30-31, 33, 34, 37,
   38-39, 40-42, 43, 44, 45, 47, 48,
   60, 61
Betar Youth movement, 20-22
Britain
   and Begin, 28, 31-35, 40, 61
   and Israeli statehood, 33
   and Palestine, 18, 30, 31-33
Brookings Institution Report, 66, 67
Brzezinski, Abigniew, 66
Bush, George H. W., 95

Camp David Peace Accord, 13-16, 70,
   72, 75-76, 99
Carter, Jimmy, 14-15, 65, 66-67, 69-70,
   72, 75
Chavet, Itzhak, 58-59
Czechoslovakia, 32

Dayan, Moshe, 41, 45, 48, 49, 54, 59-61,
   64-65, 69, 72, 78, 82
Deir Yassin, 32-33

East Jerusalem, 41
Egypt, 16
   and clashes with Israel, 42-43, 44,
      46, 48, 49, 52-54
   and peace process, 13-16, 52, 61,
      63, 64-65, 66-70, 72-73, 75-76,
      78, 98-99
Ehrlich, Simha, 59

Eisenhower, Dwight D., 43
Eitan, Rafael, 64, 80
Eliezer, Arieh Ben, 48
Eshkol, Levin, 46-48, 49, 51, 52

France, 43

Gahal, 45, 46, 49, 52
   See also Likud party
Gaza Strip, 43, 66, 72
Gemayel, Bashir, 83-84
Golan Heights, 51, 53, 97

Habib, Philip, 83
Hashomer Hatzair, 20
Hebrews, 16, 17
Herut (Freedom Movement), 34,
   37, 38, 41, 42, 43-45, 46, 49, 57,
   59, 99
Herzl, Theodor, 17-18, 27, 92
Herzog, Chaim, 91-92, 95
Histadrut, 30
Hitler, Adolf, 18, 22, 30
Hussein, King of Jordan, 65
Hussein, Saddam, 78

Iraq, and clashes with Israel, 78, 80
Irgun (Etzel), 31-33, 34-35, 40, 42
Isaac, 16, 17
Ishmael, 16-17
Islam, 14, 16-17
Israel
   Arab rights in, 39-40
   and arms, 32, 43
   and army, 34, 43, 46, 47, 48, 56, 64,
      79, 81, 84, 86
   and Ben-Gurion, 30-31, 34, 37, 38,
      40-42, 43, 44, 45, 48
   and government, 37-39, 45, 46-49,
      52, 54-61, 63-64, 79-80, 92-93
   and inflation, 90
   Jewish immigration to, 37, 45
   and occupied territories, 51-52
   and statehood, 14, 15, 17-18, 20,
      30-31, 32, 33

Israel Defense Forces (IDF), 34, 43, 46, 47, 48, 56, 64, 79, 81, 84, 86
Israeli Kahan Commission, 86

Jabotinsky, Vladimir Ze'ev, 20-22, 25, 27, 31, 38, 92
Jerusalem, 15, 41, 51, 98
Jewish Agency, 31
Jews/Judaism, 16, 17
   and Abraham story, 16, 17
   and Hitler, 18, 22, 30
   and immigration to Palestine, 18, 30-31
   and Poland, 18
Jordan, 16
   and clashes with Israel, 41, 42, 46, 48, 49, 53
   and peace process, 41, 65

Kadishai, Yehiel, 87, 90, 92, 95
King David Hotel, 32, 40
Kissinger, Henry, 54, 65
Knesset, 37-38, 39
Koran, 16, 17

Landau, Chaim, 38, 48
League of Nations, and Palestine, 18
Lebanon, 16
   and clashes with Israel, 76-79
Lebanon War, 80-87, 89, 99
Levy, David, 76
Liberal party, 45
Likud party, 52, 55, 56, 57-58, 59, 79, 80, 92

Ma'alot massacre, 56
Mapai (Labor party), 30, 38, 41-42, 44, 45, 46-48, 52, 57, 58, 59, 64, 80, 92, 93
Mapam, 38
Meir, Golda, 48, 49, 52, 53, 54, 60, 68
Mohammed, 16

Nasser, Gamal Abdul, 42, 43, 46-47, 52
Navon, Yitzhak, 59

N.K.V.D., 23, 26-28
Nobel Peace Prize, 73, 99

Old Testament, 16
Operation Litani, 76-78
Operation Peace for Galilee, 81-87

Palestine
   Aliza in, 28
   Arab-Israeli clashes in, 20-22, 31-35
   Arabs in, 18, 32-33
   Begin arriving in, 30
   and Ben-Gurion, 30-31
   and Britain, 18, 28, 30, 31-33
   Jewish immigration to, 18, 30-31
   partition of, 32
   and religious origins of conflict, 16-17
   See also Israel
Palestine Liberation Organization (PLO), 54, 69, 76-78, 80-87
Peace process
   with Egypt, 13-16, 52, 61, 63, 64-65, 66-70, 72-73, 78, 98-99
   with Jordan, 41, 65
   and United States, 13-16, 52, 54, 66-67, 69-70, 72, 75-76, 79, 83, 84
Peres, Shimon, 41, 45, 48, 49, 55, 92-93
Poland
   Begin's early years in, 18-22, 25
   and Soviet Union, 18, 28-30
Porath, Uri, 87, 90

Rabin, Yitzhak, 46, 49, 54, 55, 66, 95
Reagan, Ronald, 79, 83, 84
Rogers, William, 52, 65

Sabra-Shatilla massacre, 84, 86, 87
Sadat, Anwar, 14, 15, 52, 66, 67-68, 69, 70, 72, 73, 75-76, 81, 99
Shamir, Yitzhak, 82, 92, 93, 95
Sharett, Moshe, 42
Sharon, Ariel, 52, 59, 61, 64, 68, 75, 80, 81-82, 83, 84, 86, 87, 89, 99

Sinai Peninsula, 43, 44, 47, 52, 53, 72, 97
Six-Day War, 15, 46, 48, 49
Soviet Union
    and Israeli statehood, 32, 33
    and Poland, 18, 28-30
Strait of Tiran, 41
Straits of Aqaba, 47
Suez Canal, 41, 43
Syria, 16, 51, 65
    and clashes with Israel, 46, 48, 49, 52-54, 78-79, 81-87

Talmud, 17
Tamir, Shmuel, 46
Transjordan, 41, 42
    See also Jordan

United Nations
    and Israeli statehood, 33
    and partition of Palestine, 32

United States
    and arms to Israel, 43
    and Israeli statehood, 32, 33
    and peace process, 13-16, 52, 54, 65, 66-67, 69-70, 72, 75-76, 79, 83, 84

Warsaw University, 22
Weizman, Chaim, 38, 55
Weizman, Ezer, 55, 56, 59, 60, 61, 64, 69, 70, 76, 78
West Bank, 41, 51-52, 54, 58, 61, 64, 65, 66, 72, 86, 97
World War II, 25

Yadin, Yigael, 61
Yom Kippur War, 52-54

Zionism, 17-18, 20, 25, 27, 30-31, 41

page:

VIRGINIA BRACKETT holds a Ph.D. in English and teaches at the college level where she directs a scholars program and co-edits an arts journal titled *Ariel*. Her publications include more than 100 stories and articles for juveniles and adults. Books include *John Brown* and *Jeff Bezos* (Chelsea House); *Elizabeth Cary: Writer of Conscience* and *F. Scott Fitzgerald: Author of the Jazz Age* (Morgan Reynolds); *Steve Jobs* (Enslow Press) and *The Contingent Self: One Reading Life* (Purdue U.P.). She teaches creative writing in Tuscany during summer break and is at work on biographies of Sandra Cisneros and Virginia Woolf.

ARTHUR M. SCHLESINGER, jr. is the leading American historian of our time. He won the Pulitzer Prize for his book *The Age of Jackson* (1945) and again for a chronicle of the Kennedy Administration, *A Thousand Days* (1965), which also won the National Book Award. Professor Schlesinger is the Albert Schweitzer Professor of the Humanities at the City University of New York and has been involved in several other Chelsea House projects, including the series REVOLUTIONARY WAR LEADERS, COLONIAL LEADERS, and YOUR GOVERNMENT.